RAINBOWS
FLEAS AND
FLOWERS

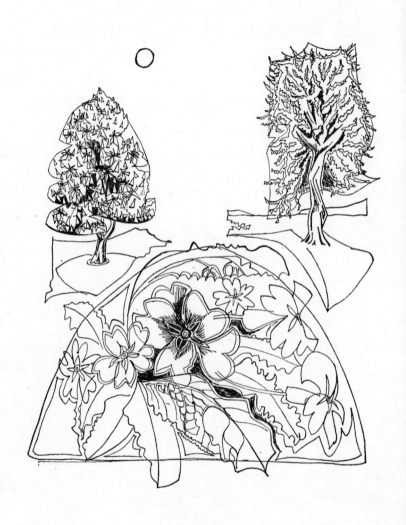

RAINBOWS
FLEAS AND
FLOWERS

A Nature Anthology

Chosen by
Geoffrey Grigson
Decorated by
Glynn Thomas

5 ROYAL OPERA ARCADE
PALL MALL LONDON SW1

© 1971, selection, introduction and commentary by
GEOFFREY GRIGSON

First published in 1971 by
JOHN BAKER (PUBLISHERS) LTD
5 Royal Opera Arcade
Pall Mall, London SW1

ISBN 0 212 98396 2

C C

PRINTED IN GREAT BRITAIN
BY W & J MACKAY LTD, CHATHAM

Contents

Hester's Book,
which she will share with
all readers

About this book

It is cheerful to learn, I think, that from space our world is an exquisite blue. Red Mars, White Venus, Blue Earth. Poets of all the past would be delighted at the news. But it would make them – if they could be persuaded into space – want all the more to turn round, and come down to go on enjoying this world, this Blue World, which is their habitat by nature.

Their world, our world, is the matter of this book; which is full of words used for the things to be seen in it, or sensed in it, if you look round and down, if you look up, by day and in the night.

Nature by itself is a large ambiguous expression. Poetry about nature, describing nature or translating it into words, or using it to describe how we think and feel about ourselves (who are nature too), is about as various as the number of poets; and such poetry is not – please notice – 'natural history'. It is not handbooks to birds, fleas, tigers, shooting stars, botany or the water supply; poets don't have to be accurate. John Clare wrote – you will find the poem on page 33 – that in the spring even 'the hoarse crow finds softer notes for love'. Tennyson wrote that in the spring 'the wanton lapwing gets itself another crest' and that 'a livelier iris changes on the burnished dove'.

Three statements which are not correct. But their seeing and hearing, their sensing, made them write what they felt in the spring, what was true to them (and is true to us). And don't forget that Wordsworth, that grave man soaked in nature and always writing about it, said that the one thing he was writing about, in fact, was Man.

As well as the obviously natural, you are going to find in this book a certain amount of nature which is in a way unnatural – creatures we have invented in natural shapes, the wild man of the woods, the phoenix, the mermaid, seals which turn into men, a crocodile king, the unicorn.

No apologies. It is as well for our brightness to have creatures in the mind; which is a kind of wild life sanctuary where they can remain unharassed and saved from extinction. There would soon be no unicorns, no mermaids, if they were 'real' (I remember seeing a mermaid wearing a tail in a freak show, arranged so that she looked as if she were in a tank. 'You big drip', one of the other show girls called her, when she was worrying about getting out in time for evening shops. We cannot be on familiar terms like that with mermaids. And all *real* mermaids would be in real tanks, or would have been hunted to extinction like dodos or Tasmanians). We cannot go unicorn-stalking or phoenix-watching – let alone shooting. Good. But nature it was, the rest of nature, which suggested such creatures to us. They deserve their place.

Often you will be reading only portions, sometimes no more than two lines, even a single line, out of a complete poem, frequently printed under a title of mine, which isn't the title of the poem it comes from. Some people who write and lay down the law about poems say that selecting and extracting pieces in that way is wrong. I don't agree with them. First of all, it often happens that we are caught only by lines, or even by no more than phrases, in a poem. And poets do frequently find an excellent kernel of words for something it is possible to hand on only in terms out of nature: they write down that kernel of words, then – art *is* knowing when to stop – they go on, they spin respectable thoughts round that experience, in more words, which may not be as good.

Frequently I have extracted (I think) these very 'true' bits from poems in which they are rather lost; believing that the scrap alone may be the real poem, and the rest fudge, or a kind of forgery. And when you look at such a piece and say it to yourself aloud, alone (as you should do with all poetry), you will find that a very short 'description' can be more than whatever it may be describing.

Japanese poets have understood that. One of them, Bashō (who lived in Charles the Second's time), said that poetry was our 'everlasting self' which we find in our daily experience. So really it is poetry – everlasting selves, including, by the way, examples of the self of Bashō – which this book offers you, in every kind of expressed detail or creature, on earth, in sea, lake, river, in snow, in frost, in the sky, and so on.

Anyhow you have only to turn to the first index, of authors, to discover what the whole poem in any such case was called. That will help you to find and read the whole poem if you wish.

Of course 'nature' isn't all of it good. I am not supposing that. So perhaps as a last word I should say this is an anthology of poems and pieces of poems prompted by enjoyable nature, mainly. If there are particular things or creatures which you like – why not? – such as rainbows or waterfalls or echoes or the Evening Star, or seals or curlews or snow, I hope you will find liking of them expressed in this book.

GEOFFREY GRIGSON

8

1 · *About our world, in general and particular*

THIS WORLD

When Amasis the King of Egypt sent to the Wise Men of Greece, to know, Quid pulcherrimum?* upon due and mature consideration they answered, The WORLD. The World certainly being so beautiful that nothing visible is capable of more. Were we to see it only once, that first appearance would amaze us. But being seen daily, we observe it not.

Thomas Traherne

THE NATURAL WORLD

I often pulled my hat over my eyes to watch the rising of the lark, or to see the hawk hang in the summer sky and the kite take its circles round the wood. I often lingered a minute on the woodland stile to hear the woodpigeons clapping their wings among the dark oaks. I hunted curious flowers in rapture and muttered thoughts in their praise. I loved the pasture with its rushes and thistles and sheep-tracks. I adored the wild, marshy fen with its solitary heronshaw sweeing along in its melancholy sky. I wandered the heath in raptures among the rabbit burrows and golden-blossomed furze. I dropt down on a thymy mole-hill or mossy eminence to survey the summer landscape . . . I marked the various colours in flat, spreading fields, checkered into closes of different-tinctured grain like the colours of a map; the copper-tinted clover in blossom; the sun-tanned green of the ripening hay; the lighter hues of wheat and barley intermixed with the sunset glare of yellow charlock and the sunset imitation of the scarlet headaches; the blue corn-bottles crowding their splendid colours in large sheets over the land and troubling the cornfields with destroying beauty; the different greens of the woodland trees, the dark oak, the paler ash, the mellow lime, the white poplars peeping above the rest like leafy steeples, the grey willow shining chilly in the sun, as if the morning mist still lingered on its cool green. I loved the meadow lake with its flags and long purples crowding the water's edge. I listened with delight to hear the wind whisper among the feather-topt reeds, to see the taper bulrush nodding in gentle curves to the rippling water; and I watched with delight on haymaking evenings the setting sun drop behind the Brigs and peep again through the half-circle of the arches as if he longed to stay . . . I observed all this with the same rapture as I have done since. But I knew nothing of poetry. It was felt and not uttered.

John Clare

---

*What is the most beautiful of things?

Scarlet 'headaches' – a common name for poppies (because of a supposi-tion that their colour and smell, if they are picked, give you a headache). Corn-bottles, or cornflowers, brilliant blue, have almost disappeared now from (English) fields of corn.

John Clare, of all English poets, of all western poets known to me, was the one most open to the life, appearances, sounds and perfumes and other qualities of the world which surrounded him. There his poetry began, so far as poetry begins outside a poet – 'But I knew nothing of poetry. It was felt and not uttered.'

There will have to be much of him in this book.

LANGUAGE OF THE EARTH

I would walk alone,
In storm and tempest, or in starlight nights
Beneath the quiet Heavens; and, at that time,
Have felt whate'er there is of power in sound
To breath an elevated mood, by form
Or image unprofaned; and I would stand,
Beneath some rock, listening to sounds that are
The ghostly language of the ancient earth,
Or make their dim abode in distant winds.

William Wordsworth

ALL THE WORLD WAS MINE

The corn was orient and immortal wheat, which never should be reaped, nor was ever sown. I thought it had stood from everlasting to everlasting. The dust and stones of the street were as precious as gold. The gates were at first the end of the world, the green trees when I saw them through one of the gates transported and ravished me; their sweetness and unusual beauty made my heart to leap, and almost mad with ecstacy, they were such strange and wonderful things: the men! O what venerable and reverend creatures did the aged seem! Immortal cherubims! And young men glittering and sparkling angels and maids strange seraphic pieces of life and beauty! Boys and girls tumbling in the street, and playing, were moving jewels. I knew not that they were born or should die . . . The city seemed to stand in Eden, or to be built in Heaven. The streets were mine, the temple was mine, the people were mine, their clothes and gold and silver were mine, as much as their sparkling eyes, fair skins and ruddy faces. The skies were mine, and so were the sun and moon and stars, and all the world was mine, and I the only spectator and enjoyer of it.

Thomas Traherne

THE COMING DAY

But now the huntsman takes his usual round
While list'ning foxes hear th' unwelcome sound;
And early peasants, who prevent the day,
May hither chance unweening guide their way;
For see – the grayish edge of dawn appears,
Night her departure mourns in dewy tears.
The goblins vanish, and the Elfin Queen
Foregoes the pleasures of the trampled green.
Nature's unwilling to be rous'd so soon,
And Earth looks pale on the declining Moon;
The nimble Hours dress out th' impatient Sun,
While rising fogs, and whisp'ring gales forerun.
The bats (a doubtful kind) begin their sleep,
And to their cells the darken'd glow-worms creep;
The coming day the conscious insects grieve,
And with slow haste the grateful herbage leave.

William Diaper

ALL THINGS ADORE GOD
IN THEIR SEASON

For ADORATION seasons change,
And order, truth, and beauty range,
    Adjust, attract, and fill:
The grass the polyanthus cheques;
And polish'd porphyry reflects,
    By the descending rill.

Rich almonds colour to the prime
For ADORATION; tendrils climb,
    And fruit-trees pledge their gems;
And Ivis, with her gorgeous vest,
Builds for her eggs her cunning nest,
    And bell-flowers bow their stems.

With vinous syrup cedars spout;
From rocks pure honey gushing out
   For ADORATION springs:
All scenes of painting crowd the map
Of nature; to the mermaid's pap
   The scalèd infant clings.

The spotted ounce and playsome cubs
Run rustling 'mongst the flow'ring shrubs,
   And lizards feed the moss;
For ADORATION beasts embark,
While waves upholding halcyon's ark
   No longer roar and toss.

               Christopher Smart

I think the polyanthus checkering the grass is the Bird's Eye Primrose, several rose-lilac flowers to every stem, which grows in limestone dells near, for instance, Christopher Smart's home in County Durham; the polish'd porphyry is the limestone so smoothly polished by waterfalls in such districts. 'To the prime' in the next stanza means to perfection. Ivis is the humming-bird, and halcyon's ark is the nest which the fabulous halcyon made on the winter sea, which it calmed.

THE SPLENDOUR FALLS ON CASTLE WALLS

The splendour falls on castle walls
   And snowy summits old in story;
The long light shakes across the lakes,
   And the wild cataract leaps in glory.
Blow, bugle, blow, set the wild echoes flying,
Blow, bugle; answer, echoes, dying, dying, dying.

O, hark, O, hear! how thin and clear
   And thinner, clearer, farther going!
O sweet and far from cliff and scar
   The horns of Elfland faintly blowing!
Blow, let us hear the purple glens replying;
Blow, bugle; answer, echoes, dying, dying, dying.

O love, they die in yon rich sky,
  They faint on hill or field or river:
Our echoes roll from soul to soul,
  And grow for ever and for ever.
Blow, bugle, blow, set the wild echoes flying,
And answer, echoes, answer, dying, dying, dying.

Alfred Tennyson

The splendour – of the evening light, yes; but of the light, too, which shows the world. Tennyson came to write this echo poem because he had just been rowed on the lakes at Killarney, in Ireland. The boatman had blown a bugle at the mountains, and the mountains sent back the long clear echo. This is still done, and it is done as well from the boats on the Königsee inside the Bavarian Alps, where I have heard it. The returning notes are more thrilling – and sad? – than you can imagine beforehand, as if the mountains were bugling. Listen to Tennyson's poem, with the French horn for the bugle, in Benjamin Britten's *Suite for Tenor, Horn and Strings.*

Tennyson said that the mountain gave back eight distinct echoes when the bugle was sounded.

THE LANDSCAPE

Straight mine eye hath caught new pleasures
Whilst the lantskip round it measures,
Russet lawns, and fallows gray,
Where the nibbling flocks do stray,
Mountains on whose barren breast
The labouring clouds do often rest:
Meadows trim with daisies pied,
Shallow brooks, and rivers wide.
Towers, and battlements it sees
Bosom'd high in tufted trees,
Where perhaps some beauty lies,
The cynosure of neighbouring eyes.
Hard by, a cottage chimney smokes,
From betwixt two aged oaks.

John Milton

CITY AND STREAM AND FIELDS

Not wholly in the busy world, nor quite
Beyond it, blooms the garden that I love.
News from the humming city comes to it
In sound of funeral or of marriage bells;
And, sitting muffled in dark leaves you hear
The windy clanging of the minster clock;
Although between it and the garden lies
A league of grass, washed by a slow broad stream,
That, stirred with languid pulses of the oar,
Waves all its lazy lilies, and creeps on,
Barge-laden, to three arches of a bridge
Crowned with the minster-towers.
                          The fields between
Are dewy-fresh, browsed by deep-uddered kine,
And all about the large lime feathers low,
The lime a summer home of murmurous wings.

Alfred Tennyson

SLIGO AND MAYO

In Sligo the country was soft, there were turkeys
    Gobbling under sycamore trees
And the shadows of clouds on the mountains moving
    Like browsing cattle at ease.

And little distant fields were sprigged with haycocks
    And splashed against a white
Roadside cottage a welter of nasturtium
    Deluging the sight.

And pullets pecking the flies from around the eyes of heifers
    Sitting in farmyard mud
Among hydrangeas and the falling ear-rings
    Of fuchsias red as blood.

But in Mayo the tumbledown walls went leap-frog
    Over the moors,
The sugar and salt in the pubs were damp in the casters
    And the water was brown as beer upon the shores

Of desolate loughs, and stumps of hoary bog-oak
　　Stuck up here and there
And as the twilight filtered on the heather
　　Water-music filled the air,

And when the night came down upon the bogland
　　With all-enveloping wings
The coal-black turfstacks rose against the darkness
　　Like the tombs of nameless kings.

Louis MacNeice

BERMUDAS

Where the remote Bermudas ride
In th'ocean's bosom unespied,
From a small boat, that row'd along,
The listning winds receiv'd this song.
　What should we do but sing his praise
That led us through the watry maze,
Unto an isle so long unknown,
And yet far kinder than our own?
Where he the huge sea-monsters wracks,
That lift the deep upon their backs.
He lands us on a grassy stage;
Safe from the storm's, and prelate's rage.
He gave us this eternal spring,
Which here enamels everything;
And sends the fowls to us in care,
On daily visits through the air.
He hangs in shades the orange bright,
Like golden lamps in a green night.
And does in the pomgranates close
Jewels more rich than Ormus shows.
He makes the figs our mouths to meet;
And throws the melons at our feet.
But apples★ plants of such a price
No tree could ever bear them twice.
With cedars, chosen by his hand,
From Lebanon, he stores the land.

★Apples: i.e. pineapples.

And makes the hollow seas, that roar,
Proclaim the ambergris on shore.
He cast (of which we rather boast)
The Gospel's pearl upon our coast.
And in these rocks for us did frame
A temple, where to sound his name.
Oh let our voice his praise exalt,
Till it arrive at heaven's vault:
Which thence (perhaps) rebounding, may
Echo beyond the Mexique Bay.
Thus sung they, in the English boat,
An holy and a cheerful note,
And all the way, to guide their chime,
With falling oars they kept the time.

Andrew Marvell

GREEN SUSSEX

You came, and looked and loved the view
  Long-known and loved by me,
Green Sussex fading into blue
  With one gray glimpse of sea.

Alfred Tennyson

DEIRDRE REMEMBERS A SCOTTISH GLEN

Glen of fruits and fish and lakes,
peaked hill of lovely wheat,
it is distressful for me to think on it,
glen full of bees, of the longhorned wild oxen.

Glen of cuckoos and thrushes and blackbirds,
precious is its cover to every fox;
glen full of wild garlic and watercress and woods,
of shamrock and flowers, leafy and twisting-crested.

Sweet are the bellings of the brown-backed dappled deer
under the oakwood over the bare hill top,
gentle hinds that are timid
lying hidden in the great-treed glen.

17

Glen of the rowan trees with scarlet berries
with fruit praised by every flock of birds,
a slumbrous paradise for the badgers
in their quiet burrows with their young.

Glen of the blue-eyed hardy hawks,
glen abounding in every fruit,
glen of the ridged and jagged peaks,
glen of blackberries and sloes and apples.

Glen of the sleek brown round-faced otters
that are pleasant and active in fishing,
many are the white-winged stately swans,
and salmon breeding along the rocky brink.

Glen of the tangled branching yews,
dewy glen with level lawn of kine,
chalk-white starry sunny glen,
glen of graceful pearl-like virtuous women.

Anon (from the medieval Irish)

A poem made about six hundred years ago, imagining Deirdre, the
most beautiful girl in all Ireland: she remembers how happy she and
Naisi her lover had been in their exile in the land of Alba, which was
Scotland – before Naisi was killed, and herself brought back to Concho-
bar, with her hands tied at her back; after which she lived for a year,
and 'In that time she never gave one smile, nor took enough food or
sleep, nor lifted up her head from her knees'.

THE RETIREMENT

I

Farewell, thou busy world, and may
   We never meet again:
Here can I eat, and sleep, and pray,
And do more good in one short day,
   Than he who his whole age out wears
   Upon the most conspicuous theatres,
Where nought but vice and vanity do reign.

II

Good God! how sweet are all things here!
How beautiful the fields appear!
How cleanly do we feed and lie!
Lord! what good hours do we keep!
How quietly we sleep!
What peace, what unanimity!
How innocent from the lewd fashion
Is all our bus'ness, all our conversation!

III

Oh how happy here's our leisure!
Oh how innocent our pleasure!
Oh ye valleys, oh ye mountains!
Oh ye groves and crystal fountains,
How I love at liberty,
By turns to come and visit ye!

IV

O Solitude, the soul's best friend,
That man acquainted with himself dost make,
And all his Maker's wonders to intend;
With thee I here converse at will,
And would be glad to do so still;
For it is thou alone, that keep'st the soul awake.

V

How calm and quiet a delight
It is, alone
To read, and meditate, and write,
By none offended, nor offending none;
To walk, ride, sit, or sleep at one's own ease,
And pleasing a man's self, none other to displease!

VI

Oh my beloved nymph! fair Dove,
Princess of rivers, how I love
Upon thy flow'ry banks to lie,
And view thy silver stream,

When gilded by a summer's beam!
And in it, all thy wanton fry
 Playing at liberty,
And with my angle upon them
 The all of treachery
I ever learn'd to practise and to try!

Such streams Rome's yellow Tiber cannot show,
Th' Iberian Tagus, nor Ligurian Po;
 The Meuse, the Danube, and the Rhine,
Are puddle-water all compar'd with thine;
And Loire's pure streams yet too polluted are
 With thine much purer to compare:
The rapid Garonne, and the winding Seine
 Are both too mean,
 Beloved Dove, with thee
 To vie priority;
Nay, Tame and Isis, when conjoin'd, submit,
And lay their trophies at thy silver feet.

Oh my beloved rocks! that rise
To awe the earth, and brave the skies,
From some aspiring mountain's crown
 How dearly do I love,
 Giddy with pleasure, to look down,
And from the vales to view the noble heights above!

Oh my beloved caves! from dog-star heats,
And hotter persecution safe retreats,
What safety, privacy, what true delight,
 In the artificial night,
 Your gloomy entrails make,
 Have I taken, do I take!
 How oft, when grief has made me fly
 To hide me from society,
 Even of my dearest friends, have I
 In your recesses' friendly shade
 All my sorrows open laid,
And my most secret woes entrusted to your privacy!

Lord! would men let me alone,
What an over-happy one
Should I think my self to be,
Might I in this desert place,
Which most men by their voice disgrace,
Live but undisturb'd and free!
Here in this despis'd recess
Would I maugre winter's cold,
And the summer's worst excess,
Try to live out to sixty full years old,
And all the while
Without an envious eye
On any thriving under Fortune's smile,
Contented live, and then contented die.

Charles Cotton

The English civil war was fought when Charles Cotton was a boy, he hated London, recollections of fighting, and strict life under Cromwell; and his river Dove, in Derbyshire, between hills of limestone in which there are caves, *is* one of the delightful rivers of the world.

DAYS THAT HAVE BEEN

Can I forget the sweet days that have been,
    When poetry first began to warm my blood;
When from the hills of Gwent I saw the earth
    Burned into two by Severn's silver flood.

When I would go alone at night to see
    The moonlight, like a big white butterfly,
Dreaming on that old castle near Caerleon,
    While at its side the Usk went softly by:

When I would stare at lovely clouds in Heaven,
    Or watch them when repeated by deep streams;
When feeling pressed like thunder, but would not
    Break into that grand music of my dreams?

Can I forget the sweet days that have been,
   The villages so green I have been in;
Llantarnam, Magor, Malpas, and Llanwern,
   Liswery, old Caerleon, and Alteryn?

Can I forget the banks of Malpas Brook,
   Or Ebbw's voice in such a wild delight,
As on he dashed with pebbles in his throat,
   Gurgling towards the sea with all his might?

Ah, when I see a leafy village now,
   I sigh and ask it for Llantarnam's green;
I ask each river where is Ebbw's voice –
   In memory of the sweet days that have been.

                  W. H. Davies

On page 239 you will find a poem in which W. H. Davies, who was a tramp for much of his life, describes himself in a not at all flattering way – his black self, his black or almost black skin, and his large lips. He says his verse is black; and it is sometimes.

UNWATCH'D, THE GARDEN BOUGH SHALL SWAY

Unwatch'd, the garden bough shall sway,
   The tender blossom flutter down,
   Unloved, that beech will gather brown,
This maple burn itself away;

Unloved, the sunflower, shining fair,
   Ray round with flames her disk of seed,
   And many a rose-carnation feed
With summer spice the humming air;

Unloved, by many a sandy bar,
   The brook shall babble down the plain,
   At noon or when the lesser wain
Is twisting round the polar star;

Uncared for, gird the windy grove,
   And flood the haunts of hern and crake;
   Or into silver arrows break
The sailing moon in creek and cove;

Till from the garden and the wild
   A fresh association blow,
   And year by year the landscape grow
Familiar to the stranger's child;

As year by year the labourer tills
   His wonted glebe, or lops the glades;
   And year by year our memory fades
From all the circle of the hills.

Alfred Tennyson

About leaving your home, feeling that no one will watch your trees, love the flowers in your garden, love your stream, or care for the near country and shore – until others grow up and make your home into theirs.

THE PLOUGH TEAM

There came the jingling of a team,
A ploughman's voice, a clink of chain,
Slow hoofs, and harness under strain.
Up the slow slope a team came bowing,
Old Callow at his autumn ploughing,
Old Callow, stooped above the hales,
Ploughing the stubble into wales;
His grave eyes looking straight ahead,
Shearing a long straight furrow red;
His plough-foot high to give it earth
To bring new food for men to birth . . .
At top of rise the plough team stopped,
The fore-horse bent his head and cropped.
Then the chains chack, the brasses jingle,
The lean reins gather through the cringle,
The figures move against the sky,
The clay wave breaks as they go by.

John Masefield

There are some words there from the huge old vocabulary of farming. Hales are the two handles of Old Callow's plough, wales are strips, the plough-foot was a piece of wood which could be adjusted either to 'give earth' to the plough (i.e. make it plough deep) or the opposite, a cringle is a ring. To chack – but you will have guessed that – is to clink or clatter.

Horses pulling a plough and (in the next poem) a horse pulling a harrow may be something English and Americans now-a-days have never seen. They only know tractors at work. All the same John Masefield and Hardy are writing about the way we feed ourselves from the world. Thomas Hardy's poem I used to pass over because his name for it was *In the Time of 'The Breaking of Nations'*. That seemed to emphasize not what happens in the poem, but what was happening round it, elsewhere. He wrote it, perhaps re-wrote it, in the First World War, remembering a day – with the harrowing farmer and the couch burning – forty-five years before, in Cornwall, when he was in love. By leaving out his title I have brought the poem back into itself, I hope.

An Anglo-Saxon farmer would have known what he meant about couch, that weed which always returns. It has its own chemical weed-killers, but you still see heaps of its dry stems burning by fields; and calling it couch or quitch we still use the Anglo-Saxon farmers' name for it – in his mouth the name was *cwice*; which meant, as in 'the quick and the dead', always quick, always living.

ONLY A MAN HARROWING CLODS

i

Only a man harrowing clods
    In a slow silent walk
With an old horse that stumbles and nods
    Half asleep as they stalk.

ii

Only thin smoke without flame
    From the heaps of couch-grass:
Yet this will go onward the same
    Though Dynasties pass.

Yonder a maid and her wight
   Come whispering by:
War's annals will cloud into night
   Ere their story die.

                 Thomas Hardy

IF BIRTH PERSISTS

He sees the gentle stir of birth
When morning purifies the earth;
He leans upon a gate and sees
The pastures, and the quiet trees.
Low, woody hill, with gracious bound,
Folds the still valley almost round;
The cuckoo, loud on some high lawn,
Is answered from the depth of dawn;
In the hedge straggling to the stream,
Pale, dew-drenched, half-shut roses gleam;
But, where the farther side slopes down,
He sees the drowsy new-waked clown
In his white quaint-embroidered frock
Make, whistling, tow'rd his mist-wreathed flock –
Slowly, behind his heavy tread,
The wet, flowered grass heaves up its head.
Leaned on his gate, he gazes – tears
Are in his eyes, and in his ears
The murmur of a thousand years.
Before him he sees life unroll,
A placid and continuous whole –
That general life, which does not cease,
Whose secret is not joy, but peace;
That life, whose dumb wish is not missed
If birth proceeds, if things subsist;
The life of plants, and stones, and rain,
The life he craves – if not in vain
Fate gave, what chance shall not control,
His sad lucidity of soul.

                 Matthew Arnold

That 'sad lucidity of soul' – Matthew Arnold was a man of severity and sadness. He was a little afraid of liking what he liked, such as early purple orchises and fords and nightingales. Tennyson liked to be sad, but often forgot it when his taste of things carried him away – Thomas Hardy too. Others are given to finding delight: Shakespeare, Herrick, Marvell, Traherne, Clare, Dorothy Wordsworth, her brother William (though he had to fight against moodiness and melancholy), Hopkins, Walt Whitman. Delight and finding things wonderful are going to be commoner than sadness as this book goes along. You see severe Arnold saying that the secret of 'general life' is peace, not joy or delight. Perhaps. Peace, anyhow, is delightful. And of course the thought of losing the delight or the peace (when we have it) causes sadness. There will be samples of that, too. Look ahead (page 245) and see what William Cowper wrote down when he looked out and saw all the leaves coming down.

CLIMBING SNOWDEN AT NIGHT

It was a Summer's night, a close warm night,
Wan, dull and glaring, with a dripping mist
Low-hung and thick that cover'd all the sky,
Half threatening storm and rain; but on we went
Uncheck'd, being full of heart and having faith
In our tried Pilot. Little could we see
Hemm'd round on every side with fog and damp,
And, after ordinary travellers' chat
With our Conductor, silently we sank
Each into commerce with his private thoughts:
Thus did we breast the ascent, and by myself
Was nothing either seen or heard the while
Which took me from my musings, save that once
The Shepherd's Cur did to his own great joy
Unearth a hedgehog in the mountain crags
Round which he made a barking turbulent.
This small adventure, for even such it seemed
In that wild place and at the dead of night,
Being over and forgotten, on we wound
In silence as before. With forehead bent
Earthward, as if in opposition set
Against an enemy, I panted up
With eager pace, and no less eager thoughts.

Thus might we wear perhaps an hour away,
Ascending at loose distance each from each,
And I, as chanced, the foremost of the Band;
When at my feet the ground appear'd to brighten,
And with a step or two seem'd brighter still;
Nor had I time to ask the cause of this,
For instantly a Light upon the turf
Fell like a flash: I looked about, and lo!
The Moon stood naked in the Heavens, at height
Immense above my head, and on the shore
I found myself of a huge sea of mist,
Which, meek and silent, rested at my feet:
A hundred hills their dusky backs upheaved
All over this still Ocean, and beyond,
Far, far beyond, the vapours shot themselves,
In headlands, tongues, and promontory shapes,
Into the Sea, the real Sea, that seem'd
To dwindle, and give up its majesty,
Usurp'd upon as far as sight could reach.
Meanwhile, the Moon look'd down upon this shew
In single glory, and we stood, the mist
Touching our very feet; and from the shore
At distance not the third part of a mile
Was a blue chasm; a fracture in the vapour,
A deep and gloomy breathing-place through which
Mounted the roar of waters, torrents, streams
Innumerable, roaring with one voice.
The universal spectacle throughout
Was shaped for admiration and delight,
Grand in itself alone, but in that breach
Through which the homeless voice of waters rose,
That dark deep thoroughfare had Nature lodg'd
The Soul, the Imagination of the whole.

William Wordsworth

DISTANT WORLDS AND STRANGE
REMOVED CLIMES

Before the starry threshold of Jove's court
My mansion is, where those immortal shapes
Of bright aerial spirits lived inspher'd

In regions mild of calm and serene air
Amidst the Hesperian gardens on whose banks
Eternal roses grow and hyacinth
Bedew'd with nectar, and celestial songs,
And fruits of golden rind, on whose fair tree
The scaly-harnessed dragon ever keeps
His uninchanted eye; and round the verge
And sacred limits of this blissful Isle
The jealous ocean, that old river, winds
His far-extended arms till with steep fall
Half his vast flood the wide Atlantique fills
And half the slow unfadom'd Stygian pool.

John Milton

The Attendant Spirit of *Comus* speaks – in a version only preserved in a manuscript – of the islands where the sweetly singing Hesperides and the dragon Ladon guard the golden apples, out in the Western Ocean. Milton goes on to speak of 'Distant worlds and strange removed climes' and I include these lines as a vision of what we like to imagine in our journeys.

2 · *Mainly about spring, summer, sun, stars and moon*

LAST SNOW

Although the snow still lingers
Heaped on the ivy's blunt webbed fingers
And painting tree-trunks on one side,
Here in this sunlit ride
The fresh unchristened things appear,
Leaf, spathe and stem,
With crumbs of earth clinging to them
To show the way they came
But no flower yet to tell their name,
And one green spear
Stabbing a dead leaf from below
Kills winter at a blow.

Andrew Young

IN THE FIELDS OF SNOW

Green the young herbs
In the fields of snow,
Green, O, how green!

After the Japanese of Raizan

Living on northern islands, Japanese and English share many things,
rain, snow, flowers, sharp and loving experience of spring, summer,
autumn, winter. Here, then, is the first of a good many translations
from Japanese – mostly ones in a special brief form, haiku, which
Japanese poets have been writing for more than 400 years. In Japanese
each haiku has seventeen syllables, with 'no rhyme, little rhythm,
assonance, alliteration or intonation'. In a haiku there is a thought, but
the thought is the piece or scrap or moment of the world which the
poet has become aware of and made into his poem – just as you see it in
this haiku about the greenness of young leaves in the snow. The thought
begins and ends with the 'vision', with the seeing, hearing, feeling, scent-
ing. Each haiku is a piece of *now*, and of *always*.

RIDDLE

Trip trap in a gap
As many feet
As a hundred sheep

(Falling hail)

30

THE HAIL ON WITHERED LEAVES

March 18, 1798. The Coleridges left us. A cold, windy morning. Walked with them half way. On our return, sheltered under the hollies, during a hail-shower. The withered leaves danced with the hailstones.

Dorothy Wordsworth

She had the purest sense of the things which pleased her, like John Clare, and like her brother William Wordsworth, and like many Japanese poets. Nothing is more surprising, no surprise last more vividly, than her record, in her journals, of things she sensed as a girl around the Quantock Hills in Somerset and around the Lakes. Coleridge said about Dorothy Wordsworth that her ways were 'simple, ardent, impressive . . . Her information various; her eye watchful in minutest observation of Nature; and her taste a perfect electrometer.'

SPRING

Nothing is so beautiful as Spring—
    When weeds, in wheels, shoot long and lovely and lush;
    Thrush's eggs look like little low heavens, and thrush
Through the echoing timber does so rinse and wring
The ear, it strikes like lightnings to hear him sing;
    The glassy peartree leaves and blooms, they brush
    The descending blue; that blue is all in a rush
With richness; the racing lambs too have fair their fling.

Gerard Manley Hopkins

In one poem Gerard Hopkins wrote of nature as a great million-fueled bonfire – 'million-fueled nature's bonfire burns on': it is not difficult to think of it like that, a bonfire to which everything contributes, bright, wonderful (smoky as well), which goes burning on and on, never extinguished, never without fuel. He followed in this idea the ancient philosopher Heraclitus, two thousand five hundred years ago, who thought of nature as perpetual fire, of which we are bright particles.

AN APRIL DAY

O, how this spring of love resembleth
  The uncertain glory of an April Day,
Which now shows all the beauty of the sun,
  And by and by a cloud takes all away!

William Shakespeare

DEWDROPS

The dewdrops on every blade of grass are so much like silver drops that
I am obliged to stoop down as I walk to see if they are pearls, and those
sprinkled on the ivy-woven beds of primroses underneath the hazels,
whitethorns, and maples are so like gold beads that I stooped down to
feel if they were hard, but they melted from my finger. And where the
dew lies on the primrose, the violet and whitethorn leaves, they are
emerald and beryl, yet nothing more than the dews of the morning on
the budding leaves; nay, the road grasses are covered with gold and
silver beads, and the further we go the brighter they seem to shine, like
solid gold and silver. It is nothing more than the sun's light and shade
upon them in the dewy morning; every thorn-point and every bramble-
spear has its trembling ornament: till the wind gets a little brisker, and
then all is shaken off, and all the shining jewelry passes away into a
common spring morning full of budding leaves, primroses, violets,
vernal speedwell, bluebell and orchis, and commonplace objects.

John Clare

DEW ON THE SWORD AND ON THE LION

i
(Othello speaks)
Keep up your bright swords, for the dew will
  rust them.

ii
(Patroclus to Achilles)
Sweet, rouse yourself; and the weak wanton Cupid
Shall from your neck unloose his amorous fold,
And, like a dew-drop from the lion's mane
Be shook to air.

William Shakespeare

A SPRING MORNING

The Spring comes in with all her hues and smells,
In freshness breathing over hills and dells;
O'er woods where May her gorgeous drapery flings,
And meads washed fragrant by their laughing springs.
Fresh are new opened flowers, untouched and free
From the bold rifling of the amorous bee,
The happy time of singing birds is come,
And Love's lone pilgrimage now finds a home;
Among the mossy oaks now coos the dove,
And the hoarse crow finds softer notes for love.
The foxes play around their dens, and bark
In joy's excess, 'mid woodland shadows dark.
The flowers join lips below; the leaves above;
And every sound that meets the ear is Love.

John Clare

The dove in Clare's poems isn't the gently purring turtle-dove, which comes from overseas to England at the end of April or the beginning of May, the traditional dove of poetry. It is the wood-pigeon or – as Clare probably intended in *A Spring Morning*, among the old oaks – the stock-dove.

ON MAY MORNING

Now the bright morning Star, day's harbinger,
Comes dancing from the east, and leads with her
The flowry May, who from her green lap throws
The yellow cowslip, and the pale primrose.
  Hail, bounteous May, that dost inspire
  Mirth and youth, and warm desire,
  Woods and groves are of thy dressing,
  Hill and dale doth boast thy blessing,
Thus we salute thee with our early song,
And welcome thee, and wish thee long.

John Milton

SPRING FLOWERS AND THE CUCKOO

When drop-of-blood-and-foam-dapple
Bloom lights the orchard-apple
  And thicket and thorp are merry
  With silver-surfèd cherry

And azuring-over greybell makes
Wood banks and brakes wash wet like lakes
  And magic cuckoocall
  Caps, clears, and clinches all.

Gerard Manley Hopkins

Greybell is the bluebell (which in Dorset English and in poems by William Barnes is the greygle, I suppose meaning the grey-blue flower). Bluebells in poems are an English speciality, since the bluebell isn't a kind of flower which goes round the world. It grows round England and Wales and Ireland, round Brittany and Normandy; but bluebell would have to be explained to someone from America, Russia or Japan, who had never seen a wood floored with bluebells. Hopkins is the poet most physical about bluebells. In one fragment he writes of drawing them up – any bluebell picker will know what that means – in another fragment he conveys even the noise and feel of picked bluebells, of 'a juicy and jostling shock of bluebells sheaved in May'.

LONDON VERSUS EPPING FOREST

The brakes, like young stag's horns, come up in Spring,
And hide the rabbit holes and fox's den;
They crowd about the forest everywhere;
The ling and holly-bush, and woods of beach,
With room enough to walk and search for flowers;
Then look away and see the Kentish heights.
Nature is lofty in her better mood,
She leaves the world and greatness all behind;
Thus London, like a shrub among the hills,
Lies hid and lower than the bushes here.
I could not bear to see the tearing plough
Root up and steal the Forest from the poor,
But leave to Freedom all she loves, untamed,
The Forest walk enjoyed and loved by all!

John Clare

NOW WELCOM SOMER

Now welcom somer, with thy sonne softe,
That hast this wintres weders over-shake,
And driven awey the longe nightes blake!

Seynt Valentyn, that art ful hy on-lofte,
Thus singen smale foules for thy sake –
Now welcom somer, with thy sonne softe,
That hast this wintres weders over-shake.

Wel han they cause for to gladen ofte,
Sith ech of hem recovered hath his make;
Ful blisful may they singen whan they wake,
Now welcom somer, with thy sonne softe,
That hast this wintres weders over-shake,
And driven awey the longe nightes blake.

Geoffrey Chaucer

All, or nearly all the words are what you would guess them to be,
without difficulty: 'weders' is weathers, i.e. storms, 'blake' is black
(as often still in the surname, William Blake, Admiral Blake), 'over-
shake' is shaken off, 'make' is mate – each bird has chosen his mate on
St Valentine's day.

CLIMBING TO THE PUDDOCK'S NEST

The huge oaks' splintered trunks appear
When spring is in her pride
As they were whitewashed every year
Upon their northern side,
And when I clomb the puddock's nest
The side that faced the south
The dust that rubbed off gen my breast
Came bitter in my mouth.

John Clare

The nest he climbed to was a kite's. Kites or puddocks were still fairly
common in England when Clare was a boy, say in 1805 – big hawks

which circle slowly through the air showing a sharp forked tail. Clare in another poem:

> Ah, could I see a spinney nigh,
> A puddock riding in the sky
> Above the oaks with easy sail
> On stilly wings and forkèd tail.★

When toys flying at the end of a string came to England from China not long before the Civil War, we had no name for them and called them kites after these familiar soaring birds with their sharp-cut tails.

RISING OF THE SUN

i

Good morrow, masters; put your torches out:
　The wolves have prey'd; and look, the gentle day,
Before the wheels of Phoebus, round about
　Dapples the drowsy east with spots of grey.

ii

Look, the morn in russet mantle clad
Walks o'er the dew of yon high eastern hill.

iii

I with the morning's love have oft made sport,
And, like a forester, the groves may tread,
Even till the eastern gate, all fiery-red,
Opening on Neptune with fair blessed beams,
Turns into yellow gold his salt green streams.

William Shakespeare

SUNRISE IN SUMMER

The summer's morning sun creeps up the blue
O'er the flat meadows' most remotest view:
A bit at first peeps from the splendid ball,
Then more, and more, until we see it all.
And then so ruddy and so cool it lies,

★ _The Fens._

The gazer views it with unwatering eyes,
And cattle opposite its kindly shine
Seem something feeding in a land divine:
Ruddy at first, yet ere a minute's told
Its burning red keeps glowing into gold,
And o'er the fenny level richly flows,
Till seeded dock in shade a giant grows;
Then blazing bright with undefined day
He turns the morning's earnest gaze away.

John Clare

THE HOUSELESS DOWNS

(From the Shepherds' Song, Sung before Queen Anne,
on the Wiltshire Downs, June 11th, 1613)

Shine, O thou sacred Shepherds' Star,
    on silly shepherd swaines,
Greeting with joy thy blessedness
    along these champian* plains.

What! dost thou stay thy motion here?
    and does thy Grace thus grace us?
This honour we esteem next that,
    when God in Heaven shall place us.

From fair Aurora's first arise,
    till silent night begins,
The day-guide Phoebus, with his beams,
    doth scorch our tawny skins,

And Boreas' rough tempestuous blasts,
    with winter frosts and storms,
Have chang'd our habit, and our hue,
    into these ugly forms.

How dare we then (base Corydons)
    in every part unsightly,
Salute an Empress all renown'd
    with rhymes compos'd so lightly?

---

* Champian: open country, champaign.

Our comfort is, thy Greatness knows
swarth faces, coarse cloth gowns,
Are ornaments that well become
the wide, wild, houseless downs.

George Ferebe

The Queen, James the First's Anne, from Denmark, arrives high up on
the downs, on a summer evening (she had been taking the waters at
Bath, and was on her way home to London): she rises there as if she
was the Evening Star, the Shepherd's Star, which I hope was actually
shining in the sky when the village people sang this song to her. George
Ferebe, who made the music and the song, was their parson. He had
trained his singers, and dressed them up as shepherds. The Queen's
road went through a gap in Wansdyke, the ancient Anglo-Saxon
cattle-barrier across the downs. In the gap (which is still called Shep-
herd's Shore) they sang to the Queen and her courtiers who sat on the
green dyke and looked down on them as if in a natural theatre.

Anne was the queen of all queens of England whom poets most
loved (whatever some of them may have written about Queen
Elizabeth), because she had been so pretty with a skin of milk and long
yellow hair, and so gay, and fond of music and dancing and pageants
and masques, which all the great poets devised for her. At the time
everyone wished to cheer her up, since her son Prince Henry (also the
poets' favourite) had died only a short time before.

VISIONS OF THE SUMMER MORNING

I love at early morn, from new-mown swath,
    To see the startled frog his route pursue,
And mark while, leaping o'er the dripping path,
    His bright sides scatter dew;
And early lark that from its bustle flies
    To hail his matin new;
        And watch him to the skies:

And note on hedgerow baulks, in moisture sprent,
    The jetty snail creep from the mossy thorn,
With earnest heed and tremulous intent,
    Frail brother of the morn,
That from the tiny bents and misted leaves
    Withdraws his timid horn,
        And fearful vision weaves;

Or swallow heed on smoke-tanned chimney-top,
  Wont to be first unsealing Morning's eye,
Ere yet the bee hath gleaned one wayward drop
  Of honey on his thigh;
To see him seek morn's airy couch to sing,
  Until the golden sky
    Bepaint his russet wing.

John Clare

SUMMER LAND

A land of hops and poppy-mingled corn,
Little about it stirring save a brook!
A sleepy land, where under the same wheel
The same old rut would deepen year by year.

Alfred Tennyson

DOWN GOETH THE GRASS

Ay me, ay me! I sigh to see the scythe afield;
  Down goeth the grass, soon wrought to wither'd hay.
Ay me, alas! ay me, alas! that beauty needs must yield,
  And princes pass, as grass doth fade away.

Ay me, ay me! that life cannot have lasting leave,
  Nor gold take hold of everlasting joy.
Ay me, alas! ay me, alas! that time hath talents to receive,
  And yet no time can make a sure stay.

Ay me, ay me! that wit cannot have wished choice,
  Nor wish can win that will desires to see.
Ay me, alas! ay me, alas! that mirth can promise no rejoice,
  Nor study tell what afterward shall be.

Ay me, ay me! that no sure staff is given to age,
  Nor age can give sure wit that youth will take.
Ay me, alas! ay me, alas! that no counsel wise and sage
  Will shun the show that all doth mar and make.

Ay me, ay me! come Time, shear on and shake thy hay;
  It is no boot to balk thy bitter blows.
Ay me, alas! ay me, alas! come Time, take every thing away,
  For all is thine, be it good or bad that grows.

Thomas Proctor

The first line imitates the slightly sucking, seething noise of scythes sweeping into the hay.

O KING OF SHADOWS

Sun, O you hide death below
The gold and the azure of a tent
In which the flowers
Hold their council; by delights
Impenetrable you keep
Hearts from realizing
The universe to be a flaw
In not existing's purity.

Great Sun, O you sound
Existence's reveille,
Companion it with fire;
Enclose it in a sleep painted
Deceivingly with landscapes;
Inciter of those phantoms of delight
By which eyes manage to detect
The indistinctness of the soul,
O king of shadows, made of flame!

From the French of Paul Valéry

Great poets belong to the sun; which makes, warms, maintains, reveals. Paul Valéry always gave himself as much sun as possible: he was up before the sun rose every day, he liked not only the first sun, but sun at the maximum fermentation of 'the busy idleness of high noon'; saying that when he looked at the sky, 'the vast naked sky', he did so with his whole body. Creatures of the sun are poets, the Phoenix, the Lion, the Unicorn, the Snake (who is light and dark: in Valéry's poem the lines I give are spoken in the Garden of Eden by the Snake, the Devil, but remember that Lucifer who fell had been the brightest of the angels –

'Angels are bright still, though the brightest fell'*). Particular flowers of the sun, to which all flowers belong, are the Marigold, the Dandelion, the Sunflower, the Morning Glory.

THE THUNDER MUTTERS LOUDER

The thunder mutters louder and more loud,
With quicker motion hay folks ply the rake;
Ready to burst slow sails the pitch black cloud,
And all the gang a bigger haycock make
To sit beneath – the woodlands' winds awake,
The drops so large wet all thro' in an hour,
A tiny flood runs down the leaning rake.
In the sweet hay yet dry the hay folks cower
And some beneath the waggons shun the shower.

John Clare

EVENING QUATRAINS

The day's grown old, the fainting sun
Has but a little way to run,
And yet his steeds, with all his skill,
Scarce lug the chariot down the hill.

With labour spent, and thirst opprest,
While they strain hard to gain the West,
From fetlocks hot drops melted light,
Which turns to meteors in the night.

The shadows now so long do grow,
That brambles like tall cedars show,
Mole-hills seem mountains, and the ant
Appears a monstrous elephant.

A very little little flock
Shades thrice the ground that it would stock;
While the small stripling following them
Appears a mighty Polyphem.

Macbeth, IV, iii.

These being brought into the fold,
And by the thrifty master told,
He thinks his wages are well paid,
Since none are either lost, or stray'd.

Now lowing herds are each-where heard,
Chains rattle in the villain's yard,
The cart's on tail set down to rest,
Bearing on high the cuckold's crest.

The hedge is stripped, the clothes brought in,
Nought's left without should be within,
The bees are hiv'd, and hum their charm,
While every house does seem a swarm.

The cock now to the roost is prest;
For he must call up all the rest;
The sow's fast pegg'd within the sty,
To still her squeaking progeny.

Each one has had his supping mess,
The cheese is put into the press,
The pans and bowls clean scalded all,
Rear'd up against the milk-house wall.

And now on benches all are sat
In the cool air to sit and chat,
Till Phoebus, dipping in the West,
Shall lead the world the way to rest.

Charles Cotton

Another poem which is sung (see page 14) in Britten's *Suite for Tenor, Horn and Strings*. Villain in the poem is a peasant or countryman, and the cart is 'bearing on high the cuckold's crest' because the shafts are standing up in the air like horns.

OF THE DAY ESTIVALL:
NOON AND EVENING

The corbeis, and the kekling kais,
May scarce the heate abide,
Halks prunyeis on the sunnie brais,
And wedders back, and side.

With gilted eyes and open wings,
The cock his courage shawes,
With claps of joy his breast he dings,
And twentie times he crawes.

The dow with whistling wings sa blew,
The winds can fast collect,
Hir pourpour pennes turnes mony hew,
Against the sunne direct.

Now noone is went, gaine is mid-day,
The heat dois slake at last,
The sunne descends downe west away,
Fra three of clock be past.

A little cule of braithing wind,
Now softly can arise,
The warks throw heate that lay behind
Now men may enterprise.

Furth fairis the flocks to seeke their fude,
On everie hill and plaine,
Ilk labourer as he thinks gude,
Steppes to his turne againe.

The rayons of the Sunne we see,
Diminish in their strength,
The schad of everie towre and tree,
Extended is in length.

Great is the calme for everie quhair,
The wind is sitten downe,
The reik thrawes right up in the air,
From everie towre and towne.

Their firdoning the bony birds,
In banks they do begin,
With pipes of reides the jolie hirds,
Halds up the mirrie din.

The Maveis and the Philomeen,
The Stirling whissilles lowd,
The Cuschetts on the branches green,
Full quietly they crowd.

The gloming comes, the day is spent,
The Sun goes out of sight,
And painted is the occident,
With pourpour sanguine bright.

The Skarlet nor the golden threid,
Who would their beawtie trie,
Are nathing like the colour reid,
And beautie of the sky.

Our West Horizon circuler,
Fra time the Sunne be set,
Is all with rubies (as it wer)
Or Rosis reid ou'rfret.

What pleasour were to walke and see,
Endlang a river cleare,
The perfite forme of everie tree,
Within the deepe appeare?

The Salmon out of cruifs and creils
Up hailed into skowts,
The bels, and circles on the weills,
Throw lowpping of the trouts.

O then it were a seemely thing,
While all is still and calme,
The praise of God to play and sing,
With cornet and with shalme.

Alexander Hume

That is part of a sizzling summer day and evening in Scotland – full of words that can't all be guessed at (though it is a good rule to say poems in obscure English out aloud. That soon settles words such as schad or shalme). Beginning with birds, there are corbeis and kekling kais, rooks and cackling jackdaws. Then there are hawks preening themselves on sunny braes. I think the next line means that the sheep, the wethers, draw back (into the shade) and stand still side by side. The dow, the wood-pigeon, flies so fast she seems to be gathering in the wind, but you see the colours changing on her purple neck feathers. The heat dies away, though there is still heat thrown back by the works, the building which was interrupted and which men have started on again. The wind has dropped, the reik, the smoke, goes straight up in the air. Birds begin their firdoning – which is a good word – their jargoning, their warbling; and the shepherds join in, on their pipes, as if they were accompanying the Mavis, and Philomeen the nightingale (whom Alexander Hume put in out of poems, I am afraid, not out of Scottish nature), and the starling, and cushats – wood-pigeons once more – which are crowding or cooing. Then comes the sunset in a sky of blood-red purple, overfret – which is embroidered – with rubies and red roses. Last, walking by the evening river, you see salmon being taken up into skowts, flat-bottomed boats, from cruifs and creils, wicker traps in salmon weirs, while the trout leap and rise, causing bubbles (bels), and circles on the pools.

The next poem is about a summer night in Wiltshire.

A NOCTURNAL REVERIE

In such a night, when every louder wind
Is to its distant cavern safe confin'd;
And only gentle Zephyr fans his wings,
And lonely Philomel, still waking, sings;
Or from some tree, fam'd for the owl's delight,
She, hollowing clear, directs the wand'rer right:
In such a night, when passing clouds give place,
Or thinly vail the heav'n's mysterious face;
When in some river, overhung with green,
The waving moon and trembling leaves are seen;
When freshen'd grass now bears itself upright,
And makes cool banks to pleasing rest invite,
Whence springs the woodbind, and the bramble-rose,
And where the sleepy cowslip shelter'd grows;

Whilst now a paler hue the foxglove takes,
Yet chequers still with red the dusky brakes:
When scatter'd glow-worms, but in twilight fine,
Slow trivial beauties, watch their hour to shine;
Whilst Salisb'ry stands the test of every light,
In perfect charms, and perfect virtue bright:
When odours, which declin'd repelling day,
Thro' temp'rate air uninterrupted stray;
When darken'd groves their softest shadows wear,
And falling waters we distinctly hear;
When thro' the gloom more venerable shows
Some ancient fabrick, awful in repose,
While sunburnt hills their swarthy looks conceal,
And swelling haycocks thicken up the vale:
When the loos'd horse now, as his pasture leads,
Comes slowly grazing thro' th' adjoining meads,
Whose stealing pace, and lengthen'd shade we fear,
Till torn up forage in his teeth we hear:
When nibbling sheep at large pursue their food,
And unmolested kine rechew the cud;
When curlews cry beneath the village walls,
And to her straggling brood the partridge calls;
Their shortliv'd jubilee the creatures keep,
Which but endures, whilst tyrant man does sleep;
When a sedate content the spirit feels,
And no fierce light disturbs, whilst it reveals;
But silent musings urge the mind to seek
Something too high for syllables to speak;
Till the free soul to a compos'dness charm'd,
Finding the elements of rage disarm'd,
O'er all below a solemn quiet grown,
Joys in th'inferior world, and thinks it like her own:
In such a night let me abroad remain,
Till morning breaks, and all's confus'd again;
Our cares, our toils, our clamours are renew'd,
Or pleasures, seldom reach'd, again pursu'd.

Anne Finch, Countess of Winchilsea

See, from the next piece, which she must have loved, how Lady
Winchilsea borrowed from Shakespeare in *The Merchant of Venice* . . .
'In such a night', repeated several times. But she borrowed well.

IN SUCH A NIGHT

Lorenzo   The moon shines bright. In such a night as this,
When the sweet wind did gently kiss the trees,
And they did make no noise, – in such a night
Troilus methinks mounted the Troyan walls,
And sigh'd his soul towards the Grecian tents,
Where Cressid lay that night.

Jessica   In such a night
Did Thisbe fearfully o'ertrip the dew,
And saw the lion's shadow ere himself,
And ran dismay'd away.

Lorenzo   In such a night
Stood Dido with a willow in her hand
Upon the wild sea-banks, and waft her love
To come again to Carthage.

Jessica   In such a night
Medea gather'd the enchanted herbs
That did renew old Æson.

Lorenzo   In such a night
Did Jessica steal from the wealthy Jew,
And with an unthrift love did run from Venice
As far as Belmont.

Jessica   In such a night
Did young Lorenzo swear he loved her well,
Stealing her soul with many vows of faith,
And n'er a true one.

Lorenzo   In such a night
Did pretty Jessica (like a little shrew)
Slander her love, and he forgave it her.

Jessica   I would out-night you, did no body come;
But hark, I hear the footing of a man.

William Shakespeare

BEFORE THE RISING OF THE MOON

The moon is in the East, I see her not;
But to the summit of the arch of heaven
She whitens o'er the azure of the sky
With thin and milky gleams of visible light.

William Wordsworth

JAPANESE NIGHT AND MOON POEMS

i
The earth is whitish
With buckwheat flowers
Under the crescent moon.

Bashō

ii
Oh for a moon
Over the road of the messenger
Who is bringing the flowers!

Kikaku

iii
The summer moon, –
It touches
The fishing-line!

Chiyo-jo

iv
The flowers darken
But the white peony
Absorbs the moonlight.

Gyōdai

v
Note from a bell,
Note from a bird on the water,
And night grows darker.

Issa

Haiku again. Two of the writers, Bashō and Issa, are among the great poets of Japan. Bashō came into the world in 1644, which made him twenty years or so younger than such memorable poets in this book as Henry Vaughan, Andrew Marvell, Charles Cotton and Richard Lovelace. Issa, born in 1763, thirty years before John Clare, wrote poems about, for example, fireflies and mosquitoes and his own fleas. Lovingly and humorously often, Issa respected everything which lives. We shall meet these two again.

BROOK NYMPHS, AND HARVESTERS

You nymphs, call'd Naiads, of the winding brooks,
With your sedg'd crowns and ever-harmless looks,
Leave your crisp channels, and on this green land
Answer your summons; Juno does command,
Come, temperate nymphs, and help to celebrate
A contract of true love; be not too late.

You sunburnt sicklemen, of August weary,
Come hither from the furrow and be merry.
Make holiday; your rye-straw hats put on
And these fresh nymphs encounter every one
In country footing.

William Shakespeare

These lines, for me, act as the setting for one line, *You sunburnt sicklemen, of August weary*, and I know others who think it one of the most wonder-evoking lines in all Shakespeare, the essence of wheat which has darkened to a dusky orange-brown, and heat, and sunburnt harvest: that, and much more.

THE FIRST-BORN STAR

The evening comes, the fields are still.
The tinkle of the thirsty rill,
Unheard all day, ascends again;
Deserted is the half-mown plain,
Silent the swaths! the ringing wain,
The mower's cry, the dog's alarms,
All housed within the sleeping farms!
The business of the day is done,
The last-left haymaker is gone,
And from the thyme upon the height,
And from the elder-blossom white
And pale dog-roses in the hedge,
And from the mint-plant in the sedge,
In puffs of balm the night-air blows
The perfume which the day forgoes.
And on the pure horizon far,
See, pulsing with the first-born star,
The liquid sky above the hill!
The evening comes, the fields are still.

Matthew Arnold

49

THE EVENING STAR

Hesperus! the day is gone,
Soft falls the silent dew,
A tear is now on many a flower
And heaven lives in you.

Hesperus! the evening mild
Falls round us soft and sweet.
'Tis like the breathings of a child
When day and evening meet.

Hesperus! the closing flower
Sleeps on the dewy ground,
While dews fall in a silent shower
And heaven breathes around.

Hesperus! thy twinkling ray
Beams in the blue of heaven,
And tells the traveller on his way
That Earth shall be forgiven!

John Clare

TO THE EVENING STAR

Thou fair-hair'd angel of the evening,
Now, whilst the sun rests on the mountains, light
Thy bright torch of love; thy radiant crown
Put on, and smile upon our evening bed!
Smile on our loves, and, while thou drawest the
Blue curtains of the sky, scatter thy silver dew
On every flower that shuts its sweet eyes
In timely sleep. Let thy west wind sleep on
The lake; speak silence with thy glimmering eyes,
And wash the dusk with silver. Soon, full soon,
Dost thou withdraw; then the wolf rages wide,
And the lion glares thro' the dun forest:
The fleeces of our flocks are cover'd with
Thy sacred dew: protect them with thine influence.

William Blake

AN EVENING IN JUNE

June 3, 1769. Saw the planet Venus enter the disk of the sun. Just as the sun was setting the spot was very visible to the naked eye. Nightingale sings; wood-owl hoots; fern-owl chatters.

Gilbert White

HESPER AND PHOSPHOR:
EVENING AND MORNING STAR

Sad Hesper o'er the buried sun
   And ready, thou, to die with him,
   Thou watchest all things ever dim
And dimmer, and a glory done.

The team is loosen'd from the wain,
   The boat is drawn upon the shore;
   Thou listenest to the closing door,
And life is darken'd in the brain.

Bright Phosphor, fresher for the night,
   By thee the world's great work is heard
   Beginning, and the wakeful bird;
Behind thee comes the greater light:

The market boat is on the stream,
   And voices hail it from the brink;
   Thou hear'st the village hammer clink,
And see'st the moving of the team.

Sweet Hesper-Phosphor, double name
   For what is one, the first, the last,
   Thou, like my present and my past,
Thy place is changed; thou art the same.

Alfred Tennyson

THE CONSTELLATION

Fair, order'd lights – whose motion without noise
    Resembles those true joys
Whose spring is on that hill, where you do grow
    And we here taste sometimes below, –

With what exact obedience do you move
    Now beneath, and now above,
And in your vast progressions overlook
    The darkest night, and closest nook!

Some nights I see you in the gladsome East,
    Some others near the West,
And when I cannot see, yet do you shine,
    And beat about your endless line.

Silence, and light, and watchfulness with you
    Attend and wind the clue,
No sleep, nor sloth assails you, but poor man
    Still either sleeps, or slips his span.

He gropes beneath here, and with restless care,
    First makes, then hugs a snare;
Adores dead dust, sets heart on corn and grass
    But seldom doth make heav'n his glass.

Henry Vaughan

RIDDLE

A lady in a boat
With a yellow petticoat.
    (*Crescent moon*)

THE HORNÈD MOON

The hornèd Moon to shine by night,
Amongst her spangled sisters bright.

John Milton

From John Milton's version (which we know as a hymn –

> For his mercies aye endure,
> Ever faithful, ever sure)

of Psalm 136. I was beginning to write poems when I first read this psalm which was 'don by the Author at fifteen yeers old'. Milton's expression of the crescent moon and the stars became mine when I read it. I haven't found a better one since.

A MOON IN CRESCENT

i

Ere the night we rose
And sauntered home beneath a moon, that, just
In crescent, dimly rained about the leaf
Twilights of airy silver, till we reached
The limit of the hills; and as we sank
From rock to rock upon the glooming quay,
The town was hushed beneath us: lower down
The bay was oily calm; the harbour-buoy,
Sole star of phosphorescence in the calm,
With one green sparkle ever and anon
Dipt by itself, and we were glad at heart.

Alfred Tennyson

ii

A crescent moon;
As I sit in the boat,
The moonlight is on my lap.

After the Japanese of Taigi

Sit still, and see how much of the light of a very thin crescent moon you can see on yourself or on things round you. This poem recalls something else to look for, the Evening Star throwing shadows; and I remember Gilbert White watching the shadows which the Evening Star cast in his room: 'Venus sheds again her silvery light on the walls of my chamber, etc., and *shadows* very strongly.' (His *Journals*, for February 9, 1782.) Taigi and Gilbert White were contemporaries.

THE WANDRING MOON

Sweet bird that shunn'st the noise of folly,
Most musical, most melancholy!
Thee chauntress oft the woods among,
I woo to hear thy even-song;
And missing thee, I walk unseen
On the dry smooth-shaven green,
To behold the wandring Moon,
Riding near her highest noon,
Like one that had bin led astray
Through the heav'ns wide pathless way;
And oft, as if her head she bow'd,
Stooping through a fleecy cloud.

John Milton

THE SHEPHERD'S EVENING

When the fields are still,
And the tired men and dogs all gone to rest,
And only the white sheep are sometimes seen
Cross and recross the strips of moon-blanch'd green.

Matthew Arnold

ROBIN GOODFELLOW'S SONG
TO THE FAIRIES

The moon shines fair and bright,
And the owl hollows,
Mortals now take their rests
Upon their pillows;
The bats abroad likewise,
And the night raven,
Which doth use for to call
Men to Death's haven.
Now the mice peep abroad,
And the cats take them,
Now do young wenches sleep,
Till their dreams wake them.
Make a ring on the grass
With your quick measures:
Tom shall play, I will sing
For all your pleasures.   *Anon*

A CHILD SEES THE MOON

Hartley fell down and hurt himself – I caught him up crying and screaming – and ran out of doors with him. – The Moon caught his eye – he ceased crying immediately – and his eyes and the tears in them, how they glittered in the Moonlight!

S. T. Coleridge

First impressions often make the best poems – quickly put down as if no words, at any rate no after words, intervened. Later on Coleridge recalled again how his son (about a year old) had been comforted by the moon – this time at the end of his poem about nightingales:

> He knows well
> The evening-star; and once, when he awoke
> In most distressful mood (some inward pain
> Had made up that strange thing, an infant's dream),
> I hurried with him to our orchard-plot,
> And he beheld the moon, and hushed at once,
> Suspends his sobs, and laughs most silently,
> While his fair eyes, that swam with undropped tears,
> Did glitter in the yellow moon-beam!

Not so good. The prose is the better poetry.

SETTING OF THE MOON

> The wan moon sets behind the white wave,
> And time is setting with me, Oh.

Robert Burns

These were two lines Yeats kept in his head – and wonderful they are. He wrote 'there are no lines with more melancholy beauty;' and then – so take heart – he repeated them wrong, in what was almost a version of his own.* It is something all of us do. Yeats went on and repeated from Blake another favourite line of moonlight (to be found on page 58), and in his mind he had rewritten that as well.

---

*In his essay *The Symbolism of Poetry*.

THE FLOOR OF HEAVEN

How sweet the moonlight sleeps upon this bank!
Here will we sit, and let the sounds of music
Creep in our ears: soft stillness and the night
Become the touches of sweet harmony.
Sit, Jessica. Look, how the floor of heaven
Is thick inlaid with patines of bright gold:

There's not the smallest orb which thou behold'st
But in his motion like an angel sings,
Still quiring to the young-eyed cherubins, –
Such harmony is in immortal souls;
But whilst this muddy vesture of decay
Doth grossly close it in, we cannot hear it.

William Shakespeare

TWO FRAGMENTS ABOUT THE STARS

i

Above
The vast of heaven stung with brilliant stars.

ii

The stars were packed so close that night
    They seemed to press and stare
And gather in like hurdles bright
    The liberties of air.

Gerard Manley Hopkins

When Hopkins was training to become a priest in the Jesuit Order a gardener saw him staring at something in the gravel, after a shower. It was a piece of quartz glittering from sunshine. He was fascinated – most poets have always been – by the sparkle of things. Another story of him: his brother was to be married and Hopkins posted him on his wedding day an exquisitely peculiar present, some of the orange and yellow feathers from the crest of a golden-crested wren which had flown into his room and blundered round the gaslight. A third story: he was once driving in Ireland and saw the shine on a newly turned furrow behind the moving plough. So he jumped down from his jaunting-car and with the ploughman's permission drove a furrow himself, his cassock tucked up under his belt.

THE MOON

The Moon is the world's glass, in which 'twere strange,
If we saw hers, and saw not our own change.

Barten Holyday

Barten Holyday you may not have met before. He was a clergyman
at Oxford, born two years after Robert Herrick (another clergyman,
but one who had to live away from the centre of things, in Devon-
shire), in 1693. When he was nearly seventy, in the year of his death,
he published a little book, charming and sententious, *A Survey of the
World* – of the world and the things in it, especially creatures. It was
written in ten books of rhyming couplets, each couplet self-contained.

TRISTRAM'S SONG

Ay, ay, O ay – the winds that bend the brier!
A star in heaven, a star within the mere!
Ay, ay, O ay – a star was my desire,
And one was far apart, and one was near:
Ay, ay, O ay – the winds that bow the grass!
And one was water and one star was fire,
And one will ever shine and one will pass,
Ay, ay, O ay – the winds that move the mere.

Alfred Tennyson

PLANETS ON THE LAKE

Clouds, lingering yet, extend in solid bars
Through the grey west; and lo! these waters, steeled
By breezeless air to smoothest polish, yield
A vivid repetition of the stars;
Jove, Venus, and the ruddy crest of Mars
Amid his fellows beauteously revealed.

William Wordsworth

THE MOON ON GRASMERE

October 31, 1800. A very fine moonlight night – The moon shone like herrings in the water.

Dorothy Wordsworth

A MOONGLADE

And on a sudden, lo! the level lake,
And the long glories of the winter moon.

Alfred Tennyson

The poet James Russell Lowell seems to have invented 'moonglade' as a word for the long shaking paths of moonlight coming to one's feet across the sea, or a lake, or a river. Tennyson's moonglade comes into Sir Bedivere's sight, in *Morte d'Arthur*, when the Three Queens arrive for Arthur in their dusky barge.

THE FISHES AND THE MOON

Like the gay fishes on the wave, when the cold moon
    drinks the dew.

William Blake

Turn back to page 55, for Yeats and this line from one of Blake's long poems.

COMETS

Hung be the heavens with black, yield day to night!
Comets, importing change of times and states,
Brandish your crystal tresses in the sky!

William Shakespeare

The tresses of the best comets do seem like crystal in the night. When such a long-haired or long-tailed prodigy swims or hangs where it oughtn't to be against a familiar constellation, you never forget it, you understand why these interruptions in the ordered sky where thought to portend interruption of the order of things on earth, why it was supposed that kings would die or lose their kingdoms. Kepler the astronomer was of opinion that 'Comets were made, to the end that the etherial Region might not be more void of monsters than the Ocean is of Whales and other great thieving fishes.'

PRODIGIES OF THE NIGHT

Here, in the night appears a flaming spire;
There a fierce dragon folded all in fire;
Here, a bright comet; there a burning beam;
Here, flying launces; there, a fiery stream:
Here seems a horned goat, environ'd round
With fiery flakes, about the air to bound.
There, with long bloody hair, a blazing star
Threatens the world with famine, plague and war:
To princes, death: to kingdoms, many crosses;
To all estates, inevitable losses:
To herd-men, rot: to plough-men, hapless seasons:
To sailors, storms: to cities, civil treasons.

Joshua Sylvester (from the French of
Guillaume de Salluste du Bartas)

More of such monsters: All of them, in fact, comets.

Men thought the particular shape of a comet foretold disasters of a particular kind. For instance, war came after a comet shaped like a sword. Comets, all the same, could be propitious: very silvery ones 'with the clearest and purest of beams', wrote John Gadbury the astrologer, in the disturbed times of Charles I and Cromwell and Charles II, portended 'abundance of corn and fruits'.

The comet which Thomas Hardy saw, with a girl, saddened him, rather than frightened him, as you will see: it would return and the girl would be dead. Perhaps it was the Great Comet of 1861 (Thomas Hardy was twenty-one when it blazed across the English counties in July), which was truly 'cometes', or long-haired, a long-haired star, as the Greeks would have said (The Japanese thought of comets as besoms up in the sky, 'besom-stars').

THE COMET AT YELL'HAM

I
It bends far over Yell'ham Plain,
    And we, from Yell'ham Height,
Stand and regard its fiery train,
    So soon to swim from sight.

II
It will return long years hence, when
    As now its strange swift shine
Will fall on Yell'ham; but not then
    On that sweet form of thine.

Thomas Hardy

3 · *About flowers, leaves and trees*

FLOWERS OF SPRING

And out once more in varnished glory shine
Thy stars of celandine.

Alfred Tennyson

IN THE SPRING

The almond flourisheth, the birch trees flow,
The sad mezereon cheerfully does blow,
The flow'ry sons before their fathers seen,
And snails begin to crop the mandrake green,
The vernal sun with crocus gardens fills,
With hyacinths, anemones and daffodils:
The hazel catkins now delate and fall,
And paronychions peep upon each wall.

Sir Thomas Browne

'Sons before their fathers' is said of plants whose flowers come out before the leaves, such as the mezereon. Probably the mandrake which the snails are eating, is the real mandrake, legend's mandragora (of the same powerful family as Deadly Nightshade). Sir Thomas Browne was a doctor. He would have had mandrake in his garden: it came up in spring from seeds sown in the autumn, and doctors had their uses for it. Paronychions sound strange, but they are plants of the tiny whitlow grass.

THE HAWTHORN

Amongst the many buds proclaiming May,
(Decking the fields in holy-day's array,
Striving who shall surpass in bravery)
Mark the fair blooming of the hawthorn-tree,
Who finely clothed in a robe of white,
Feeds full the wanton eye with May's delight;
Yet for the bravery that she is in·
Doth neither handle card nor wheel to spin,
Nor changeth robes but twice: is never seen
In other colours than in white or green.
Learn then content, young shepherd, from this tree,
Whose greatest wealth is Nature's livery;

And richest ingots never toil to find,
Nor care for poverty but of the mind.

William Browne

THE SHEPHERDS' HAWTHORN-BUSH

Gives not the hawthorn-bush a sweeter shade
To shepherds looking on their silly sheep,
Than doth a rich embroider'd canopy
To kings that fear their subjects' treachery?
O, yes, it doth; a thousand-fold it doth,
And to conclude, the shepherd's honely curds,
His cold thin drink out of his leather bottle,
His wonted sleep under a fresh tree's shade,
All which secure and sweetly he enjoys,
Is far beyond a prince's delicates.

William Shakespeare

THE CHERRY TREE

The cherry trees bend over and are shedding,
On the old road where all that passed are dead,
Their petals, strewing the grass as for a wedding
This early May morn, though there is none to wed.

Edward Thomas

WOOD ANEMONES, BLUEBELLS, ORCHISES:
THE SCHOLAR-GIPSY COMES AND GOES

For most, I know, thou lov'st retiréd ground!
  Thee at the ferry Oxford riders blithe,
    Returning home on summer-nights, have met
  Crossing the stripling Thames at Bab-lock-hithe,
    Trailing in the cool stream thy fingers wet,
      As the punt's rope chops round;
  And leaning backward in a pensive dream,
    And fostering in thy lap a heap of flowers
    Plucked in shy fields and distant Wychwood bowers,
  And thine eyes resting on the moonlit stream.

And then they land, and thou art seen no more!
  Maidens, who from the distant hamlets come
    To dance around the Fyfield elm in May,
  Oft through the darkening fields have seen thee roam,
    Or cross a stile into the public way.
      Oft thou hast given them store
  Of flowers – the frail-leafed, white anemone,
    Dark bluebells drenched with dews of summer eves,
    And purple orchises with spotted leaves –
But none hath words she can report of thee.

And, above Godstow Bridge, when hay-time's here
  In June, and many a scythe in sunshine flames,
    Men who through those wide fields of breezy grass
  Where black-winged swallows haunt the glittering Thames,
    To bathe in the abandoned lasher pass,
      Have often passed thee near
  Sitting upon the river bank o'ergrown;
    Marked thine outlandish garb, thy figure spare,
    Thy dark vague eyes, and soft abstracted air
But, when they came from bathing, thou wast gone!

At some lone homestead in the Cumner hills,
  Where at her open door the housewife darns,
    Thou hast been seen, or hanging on a gate
  To watch the threshers in the mossy barns.
    Children, who early range these slopes and late
      For cresses from the rills,
  Have known thee eyeing, all an April-day,
    The springing pastures and the feeding kine;
    And marked thee, when the stars come out and shine,
Through the long dewy grass move slow away.

In Autumn, on the skirts of Bagley Wood –
  Where most the gipsies by the turf-edged way
    Pitch their smoked tents, and every bush you see
  With scarlet patches tagged and shreds of grey,
    Above the forest-ground called Thessaly –
      The blackbird, picking food,

Sees thee, nor stops his meal, nor fears at all;
  So often has he known thee past him stray,
  Rapt, twirling in thy hand a withered spray,
And waiting for the spark from heaven to fall.

Matthew Arnold

A SINGLE ASH

      A single Tree
There was, no doubt yet standing there, an Ash
With sinuous trunk, boughs exquisitely wreath'd;
Up from the ground and almost to the top
The trunk and master branches everywhere
Were green with ivy; and the lightsome twigs
And outer spray profusely tipp'd with seeds
That hung in yellow tassels and festoons,
Moving or still, a Favourite trimm'd out
By Winter for himself, as if in pride,
And with outlandish grace. Oft have I stood
Foot-bound, uplooking at this lovely Tree
Beneath a frosty moon. The hemisphere
Of magic fiction, verse of mine perhaps
May never tread; but scarcely Spenser's self
Could have more tranquil visions in his youth.
More bright appearances could scarcely see
Of human Forms with superhuman Powers,
Than I beheld, standing on winter nights
Alone, beneath this fairy work of earth.

William Wordsworth

THE PINE AT SHIOGESHI

All night down from the pine of Shiogeshi
Which invites the wind off the sea
To convey the saltness of the waves,
Fall glittering drops of moonlight.

After the Japanese of Saigyō

A CONTEMPLATION UPON FLOWERS

Brave flowers, that I could gallant it like you
And be as little vain!
You come abroad, and make a harmless show,
And to your beds of earth again;
You are not proud, you know your birth,
For your embroider'd garments are from earth:

You do obey your months, and times, but I
Would have it ever spring,
My fate would know no winter, never die
Nor think of such a thing;
Oh that I could my bed of earth but view
And smile, and look as cheerfully as you:

Oh teach me to see death, and not to fear
But rather to take truce;
How often have I seen you at a bier,
And there look fresh and spruce;
You fragrant flowers, then teach me that my breath
Like yours may sweeten, and perfume my death.

Henry King

FLOWERS OF THE BROOM

There for me and my sweetheart
Is life, a fresh saffron field.
I've a house, a good dwelling
Made of Arabian gold.
Tent of the firmament's Lord,
Cloth of gold, the roof's speckled;
A fair angel of heaven
Embroidered it for May's bed:
Gold gossamer, wondrous bees,
God's glow-worms, gems of sunlight.
What bliss on the vine-clad hill
To have the young twigs gilded,
And the tips of bushes seen
Like the stars, golden bullion.

Anon (from the Welsh)

Flowering in May – but not so common now as it used to be, covering and scenting stony ground and hillsides and mountain sides – broom is the plant of being in love and of the power of love in many poems of the Middle Ages and later, in many languages.

OLWEN AND THE FLOWERS

Yellower was her head than the flowers of the broom, her skin whiter than the froth of the waves; her two hands and her fingers were whiter than the flowers of the bogbean in the small gravel from a bubbling spring. The eye of a hawk caged for its moulting and the eye of the falcon at its third moulting were less bright than her eye. Her two breasts were whiter than the white swan's breast; her cheeks were redder than the foxglove. To see her filled all with love. Four white flowers of clover would spring wherever she walked. So Olwen, White Footstep, was her name.

From the Welsh of the Mabinogion

Olwen – in the *Mabinogion*, the Welsh tales written down in the tenth century, she is the daughter of the Chief Giant, Yspaddaden: Kulhwch wishes to marry her, and does so with King Arthur's help; but only after performing tasks more fantastic and numerous than the Labours of Hercules. In the end the Chief Giant has to agree, he is dragged by the hair to his own dung-heap, and his head is sliced off, and raised on a stake above his hill-fort. Olwen then goes to Kulhwch. Of course Olwen's hands and fingers should be compared with the pink-budded white flowers of the bogbean. The bogbean, the dog-rose, the foxglove, and the broom are the four most beautiful flowers of Wales. Translators have given different identities to the flowers which were less white than Olwen's hands and fingers – the wood-anemone (that is the version which was known to Yeats, who found much wonder and delight in flower passages in the *Mabinogion*), the bladder-campion, the melilot; but bogbean is the right flower, I think. It fits the small gravel from the bubbling spring – and it fits Olwen as well.

   In Irish and Welsh writing girls are often given cheeks like the foxglove.

THE FOXGLOVE

The Foxglove, one by one,
Had shed its bells, and stood by the wayside
Dismantled, with a single one, perhaps,
Left at the ladder's top, with which the Plant
Appeared to stoop, as slender blades of grass
Tipp'd with a bead of rain or dew.

William Wordsworth

THE MARIGOLD

The Marigold whose courtier's face
Echoes the Sun and doth unlace
Her at his rise, at his full stop
Packs and shuts up her gaudy shop.

John Cleveland

THE FEAR OF FLOWERS

(The Thistle)

The nodding oxeye bends before the wind,
The woodbine quakes lest boys their flowers should find,
And prickly dog-rose, spite of its array,
Can't dare the blossom-seeking hand away,
While thistles wear their heavy knobs of bloom
Proud as a war-horse wears its haughty plume,
And by the roadside danger's self defy,
On commons where pined sheep and oxen lie,
In ruddy pomp and ever thronging mood
It stands and spreads like danger in a wood.
And in the village street, where meanest weeds
Can't stand untouched to fill their husks with seeds.
The haughty thistle o'er all danger towers,
In every place the very wasp of flowers.

John Clare

SONNET

Leaves of the summer, lovely summer's pride,
　Sweet is the shade below your silent tree,
Whether in waving copses, where ye hide
　My roamings, or in fields that let me see
　The open sky; and whether ye may be
Around the low-stemm'd oak, robust and wide;
Or taper ash upon the mountain side;
　Or lowland elm; your shade is sweet to me.

Whether ye wave above the early flow'rs
　In lively green; or whether, rustling sere,
　Ye fly on playful winds, around my feet,
In dying autumn; lovely are your bow'rs,
　Ye early dying children of the year;
　Holy the silence of your calm retreat.

William Barnes

RIDDLES

i

The thousand children beautiful of this my body bred,
Both sons and daughters finely decked, I live, and they are dead.
My sons were put to extreme death by such as loved them well,
My daughters died with extreme age, but where I cannot tell.
　　(*An apple tree, whose sons are apples and
　　daughters leaves*)

ii

On yonder hill there is a deer
Reaching from here to Lancashire,
East, west, north, south,
Five thousand teeth and never a mouth.

(*Gorse*)

The riddle about the prickly gorse comes from the Midlands, where
gorse is always gorse. Coleridge, in the next two lines, calls it furze.
But then he came from Devonshire (like Sir Walter Ralegh, he kept

69

something of a Devonshire accent) and in Devonshire, Cornwall, Somerset, Dorset (and much of Ireland) furze is the proper word. William Barnes – as a Dorset poet – calls it furze, or rather vuzz. John Clare, belonging to Northamptonshire in the Midlands, calls it goss.

THE PERFUME OF THE FURZE

Now the gentle dew-fall sends abroad
The fruit-like perfume of the golden furze.

S. T. Coleridge

SEVEN SIMPLES

And can the physician make sick men well,
And can the magician a fortune divine,
Without lily, germander, and sops-in-wine?
    With sweetbriar
    And bonfire,
    And strawberry wire,
    And columbine.

Within and out, in and out, round as a ball,
With hither and thither, as straight as a line,
With lily, germander, and sops-in-wine,
    With sweetbriar,
    And bonfire,
    And strawberry wire,
    And columbine.

When Saturn did live, there lived no poor,
The king and the beggar with roots did dine,
With lily, germander, and sops-in-wine,
    With sweetbriar,
    And bonfire,
    And strawberry wire,
    And columbine.

Anon

Simples are simple or single ingredients of a medicine, and I have called this nameless poem of Herrick's time *Seven Simples* to get its atmosphere right. Poets then were beginning to enjoy the names of flowers, which

70

were beginning to be grown for themselves as well as for their uses. Sops-in-wine (a sop is something soaked) are clove pinks. Bonfire is probably the daisy, the banflower or bone-flower, and strawberry wire is a strawberry runner.

MEADOWS

In yellow meadows I take no delight.
Let me have those which are most red and white.

Sir Thomas Browne

TO MEADOWS

Ye have been fresh and green,
    Ye have been fill'd with flowers:
And ye the walks have been
    Where maids have spent their hours.

You have beheld, how they
    With wicker arks did come
To kiss, and bear away
    The richer cowslips home.

Y'ave heard them sweetly sing,
    And seen them in a round:
Each virgin, like a spring,
    With honeysuckles crown'd.

But now we see none here,
    Whose silv'ry feet did tread,
And with dishevell'd hair,
    Adorn'd this smoother mead.

Like unthrifts, having spent
    Your stock, and needy grown,
Y'are left here to lament
    Your poor estates, alone.

Robert Herrick

Honeysuckles here are flowers of clover.

COWSLIPS BY A STREAM

Cowslips, like topazes which shine,
Close by the silver serpentine.

Christopher Smart

THE BINDWEED

The bindweed roots pierce down
    Deeper than men do lie,
Laid in their dark-shut graves
    Their slumbering kinsmen by.

Yet what frail thin-spun flowers
    She casts into the air,
To breathe the sunshine, and
    To leave her fragrance there.

But when the sweet moon comes,
    Showering her silver down,
Half-wreathed in faint sleep,
    They droop where they have blown.

So all the grass is set,
    Beneath her trembling ray,
With buds that have been flowers,
    Brimmed with reflected day.

Walter de la Mare

WITHWIND

The unprofitable bindweed spread his bells
From side to side, and with unwieldy wreaths
Had dragged the rose from its sustaining wall
And bent it down to earth.

William Wordsworth

I have put Withwind above these four lines by Wordsworth because
that was the name by which the first English knew a plant which is
both exquisite and hateful to gardeners. Withwind is still the name used
in southern English counties for the small bindweed with pink striped

flowers and the delicate scent which Walter de la Mare notices, and for the larger bindweed with white flowers, which has exactly that dragging unwieldy effect in a garden. Wordsworth is writing about the neglected garden of a cottage.

POPPIES AND BINDWEED

Through the thick corn the scarlet poppies peep,
And round green roots and yellowing stalks I see
　　Pale pink convolvulus in tendrils creep;
　　　　And air-swept lindens yield
Their scent, and rustle down their perfumed showers
　　Of bloom on the bent grass where I am laid.
　　And bower me from the August sun with shade.

Matthew Arnold

Corn – by English usage wheat or barley or oats – and in the corn, though less and less in modern times, brilliant poppies. Hopkins is the English poet who makes the most brilliant poppies – poppies 'in the blue wheat-acre', which are 'crush-silk' and 'aflash', each one having its

　　　　　　blood-gash blade-gash
　　　Flame-rash rudred
　　　Bud shelling

or its

　　　　　　bread-shed
　　　Tatter-tassel-tangled and dingle-a-danglèd
　　　Dandy-hung dainty head.★

ROSES OF SUMMER AND AUTUMN

i
(The Princes in the Tower)

Their lips were four red roses on a stalk,
Which in their summer beauty kiss'd each other.

ii
　　　　　. . . hoary-headed frosts
Fall in the fresh lap of the crimson rose.

William Shakespeare

★In the fragment called *The Woodlark*.

THE ROSE

The Rose is but the flower of a briar:
The Good Man has an Adam to his sire.

Barten Holyday

THE SICK ROSE

O Rose, thou art sick!
The invisible worm
That flies in the night,
In the howling storm,

Has found out thy bed
Of crimson joy,
And his dark secret love
Does thy life destroy.

William Blake

VIRTUE

Sweet day, so cool, so calm, so bright,
The bridal of the earth and sky:
The dew shall weep thy fall to-night;
   For thou must die.

Sweet rose, whose hue angry and brave
Bids the rash gazer wipe his eye:
Thy root is ever in its grave,
   And thou must die.

Sweet spring, full of sweet days and roses,
A box where sweets compacted lie;
My music shows ye have your closes,
   And all must die.

Only a sweet and virtuous soul,
Like season'd timber, never gives;
But though the whole world turn to coal,
   Then chiefly lives.

George Herbert

74

MORNING GLORIES

(from Japan)

i

A single Morning Glory
The colour
Of a deep pool.

Busōn

ii

Morning Glories
Growing towards
The scorching pebbles.

Issa

iii

My hut!
Thatched with the flowers
Of the Morning Glory.

Issa

Morning Glories have earned poems in Japan like roses with us. No wonder. You can stare into them as if they were blue pools of water in limestone or blue swimming pools – or you can let them stare at you. Each flower lasts only a day. In America and Japan people are lucky, it is hot enough in summer for Morning Glories to grow and climb quickly. In France, south of Normandy which is more English, Morning Glories will seed themselves and come up year after year. In England they need coddling, and even then they want more than a usually good summer.

It is the Americans who invented the English name Morning Glory, in itself a poem. The Japanese call the Morning Glory *asagao*, and their poems about it traditionally belong to the autumn – I mean their haiku, their very short poems. Each haiku has a season word, and *asagao* or Morning Glory is such a word. To be sure there is something specially autumnal about Morning Glories in our feeling, so I shall include one or two more *asagao* poems later on in the section of this book which goes from autumn to winter.

ORANGE BUDS BY MAIL FROM FLORIDA

(Voltaire closed a famous argument by claiming that a ship of war and the grand opera were proofs enough of civilization's and France's progress, in his day.)

A lesser proof than old Voltaire's, yet greater,
Proof of this present time, and thee, thy broad expanse, America,
To my plain Northern hut, in outside clouds and snow,
Brought safely for a thousand miles o'er land and tide,
Some three days since on their own soil live-sprouting,
Now here their sweetness through my room unfolding,
A bunch of orange buds by mail from Florida.

Walt Whitman

MADONNA LILY

O lovely lily clean,
O lily springing green,
O lily bursting white.

John Masefield

A writer on Japanese poems (he translated most of the ones you find in this book) has written that these three lines are like a haiku in English. They are part of an exclamation which finishes off a very long poem about religion and nature. If they are the lily of religion, they are more than a church lily embroidered in white on green: they *are* the Madonna lily in the garden opening from green to white.

THE QUEST OF THE PURPLE-FRINGED

I felt the chill of the meadow underfoot,
But the sun overhead;
And snatches of verse and song of scenes like this
I sung or said.

I skirted the margin alders for miles and miles
In a sweeping line.
The day was the day by every flower that blooms,
But I saw no sign.

Yet further I went to be before the scythe,
For the grass was high;
Till I saw the path where the slender fox had come
And gone panting by.

Then at last and following him I found –
In the very hour
When the colour flushed to the petals it must have been –
The far-sought flower.

There stood the purple spires with no breath of air
Nor headlong bee
To disturb their perfect poise the livelong day
'Neath the alder tree.

I only knelt and putting the boughs aside
Looked, or at most
Counted them all to the buds in the copse's depth
That were pale as a ghost.

Then I arose and silently wandered home,
And I for one
Said that the fall might come and whirl of leaves,
For summer was done.

Robert Frost

STONE-PIT

The passing traveller with wonder sees
A deep and ancient stone-pit full of trees,
So deep and very deep the place has been,
The church might stand within and not be seen.
The passing stranger oft with wonder stops
And thinks he e'en could walk upon their tops,
And often stoops to see the busy crow,
And stands above and sees the eggs below;
And while the wild horse gives its head a toss,
The squirrel dances up and runs across.
The boy that stands and kills the black-nosed bee
Dares down as soon as magpies' nest are found,
And wonders when he climbs the highest tree
To find it reaches scarce above the ground.

John Clare

THE MOUNTAIN-ASH

                    The Mountain-ash
No eye can overlook, when 'mid a grove
Of yet unfaded trees she lifts her head
Decked with autumnal berries, that outshine
Spring's richest blooms; and ye may have marked,
By a brook-side or solitary tarn,
How she her station doth adorn: the pool
Glows at her feet, and all the gloomy rocks
Are brightened round her.

                              William Wordsworth

Making the mountain-ash a she and giving her feet and saying that
she adorns her station – I agree that is not grave William Wordsworth
at his happiest. But then comes the pool glowing from the (scarlet)
berries. And the brightening of the rocks. Wordsworth recovers. It is
also wonderful to come on a mountain-ash by itself on moorland with
all its berries fixed in the frost blue of a morning in November. But
Wordsworth's tree is more subtle, because it looks to me as if he was
seeing in his mind a particular mountain-ash brilliant in a day which
was overcast and dull, in the declining year.

THE SPINDLE TREE

As full of berries as its twigs can be,
Glittering and pink as blossoms washed in dew
Gleams the gay burthen of the spindle tree.
The Old Man's Beard the sapling's grains* pursues
Like feathers hung with rime, but autumn's showers
Makes their rich berries shine like summer flowers.

                              John Clare

A GREEN PLUM

Fair creature, kill'd too soon by death's sharp sting!
Like a green plum that hangs upon a tree,
    And falls, through wind, before the fall should be.

                              William Shakespeare

---

*Grains: main branches.

RIPE MULBERRIES

Now humble as the ripest mulberry
That will not hold the handling.

William Shakespeare

SEEDS IN THE AIR

September 1, 1800. The beards of thistle and dandelions flying above
the lonely mountains like life, and I saw them thro' the trees skimming
the lake like swallows.

S. T. Coleridge

A LATE WALK

When I go up through the mowing field,
    The headless aftermath,
Smooth-laid like thatch with the heavy dew,
    Half closes the garden path.

And when I come to the garden ground,
    The whir of sober birds
Up from the tangle of withered weeds
    Is sadder than any words.

A tree beside the wall stands bare,
    But a leaf that lingered brown,
Disturbed, I doubt not, by my thought,
    Comes softly rattling down.

I end not far from my going forth
    By picking the faded blue
Of the last remaining aster flower
    To carry again to you.

Robert Frost

My father who found the English landscape tame
Had hardly in his life walked in a wood,
Too old when first he met one; Malory's knights,
Keats's nymphs or the Midsummer Night's Dream
Could never arras the room, where he spelled out True and Good,
With their interleaving of half-truths and not-quites.

While for me from the age of ten the socketed wooden gate
Into a Dorset planting, into a dark
But gentle ambush, was an alluring eye;
Within was a kingdom free from time and sky,
Caterpillar webs on the forehead, danger under the feet,
And the mind adrift in a floating and rustling ark

Packed with birds and ghosts, two of every race,
Trills of love from the picture-book – Oh might I never land
But here, grown six foot tall, find me also a love
Also out of the picture-book; whose hand
Would be soft as the webs of the wood and on her face
The wood-pigeon's voice would shaft a chrism from above.

So in a grassy ride a rain-filled hoof-mark coined
By a finger of sun from the mint of Long Ago
Was the last of Lancelot's glitter. Make-believe dies hard;
That the rider passed here lately and is a man we know
Is still untrue, the gate to Legend remains unbarred,
The grown-up hates to divorce what the child joined.

Thus from a city when my father would frame
Escape, he thought, as I do, of bog or rock
But I have also this other, this English, choice
Into what yet is foreign; whatever its name
Each wood is the mystery and the recurring shock
Of its dark coolness is a foreign voice.

Yet in using the word tame my father was maybe right,
These woods are not the Forest; each is moored
To a village somewhere near. If not of to-day
They are not like the wilds of Mayo, they are assured
Of their place by men; reprieved from the neolithic night
By gamekeepers or by Herrick's girls at play.

And always we walk out again. The patch
Of sky at the end of the path grows and discloses
An ordered open air long ruled by dyke and fence,
With geese whose form and gait proclaim their consequence,
Pargetted outposts, windows browed with thatch,
And cow pats – and inconsequent wild roses.

                                    Louis MacNiece

O SWEET WOODS

O sweet woods, the delight of solitariness!
O how much I do like your solitariness!
Where man's mind hath a freed consideration
Of goodness to receive lovely direction;
Where senses do behold th' order of heav'nly host,
And wise thoughts do behold what the Creator is.
Contemplation here holdeth his only seat,
Bounded with no limits, born with a wing of hope,
Climbs even unto the stars; Nature is under it.
Nought disturbs thy quiet, all to thy service yields:
Each sight draws on a thought (thought, mother of science);
Sweet birds kindly do graunt harmony unto thee;
Fair trees' shade is enough fortification,
Nor danger to thy self if it be not in thy self.

O sweet woods, the delight of solitariness!
O how much I do like your solitariness!
Here nor treason is hid, veiled in innocence,
Nor envy's snaky eye finds any harbour here,
Nor flatterers' venomous insinuations,
Nor cunning humourists' puddled opinions,
Nor courteous ruin of proffered usury,
Nor time prattled away, cradle of ignorance,
Nor causeless duty, nor cumber of arrogance,
Nor trifling title of vanity dazzleth us,
Nor golden manacles stand for a paradise.
Here wrong's name is unheard, slander a monster is.
Keep thy spright from abuse; here no abuse doth haunt.
What man grafts in a tree dissimulation?

O sweet woods, the delight of solitariness!
O how well do I like your solitariness!
Yet, dear soil, if a soul closed in a mansion
As sweet as violets, fair as lily is,
Straight as cedar, a voice stains the canary bird's,
Whose shade safely doth hold, danger avoideth her;
Such wisdom that in her lives speculation;
Such goodness that in her simplicity triumphs;
Where envy's snaky eye winketh or else dieth;
Slander wants a pretext, flattery gone beyond;
Oh! if such a one have bent to a lonely life,
Her steps glad we receive, glad we receive her eyes,
   And think not she doth hurt our solitariness,
   For such company decks such solitariness.

Sir Philip Sidney

He does wander away, I agree, from the 'sweet woods'. Yet back they
come with each new division of his poem; and we remember from it
the refrain, and the long 'solitariness', which chimes in the poem eight
times.

NAY, IVY, NAY

Nay! Ivy, nay!
It shall not be, iwis:
Let Holly have the maistry,
As the manner is.

Holly stond in the hall
Fair to behold:
Ivy stond without the door –
She is full sore acold.

Holly and his merry men
They daunsen and they sing;
Ivy and her maidens
They weepen and they wring.

Ivy hath a kibe –
She caught it with the cold.
So mot they all have aye
That with Ivy hold.

Holly hath berries
As red as any rose:
The foster, the hunters
Keep them fro the does.

Ivy hath berries
As black as any sloe:
There come the owl
And eat them as she go.

Holly hath birds,
A full fair flock:
The nightingale, the poppinguy,
The gentle laverock.

Good Ivy, good Ivy,
What birds hast thou?
None but the owlet
That cry How! How!

Anon (Fifteenth century)

Some words, first of all. Iwis is indeed, stond means stands and to wring is to suffer. A kibe is a chilblain, a foster a forester, looking after the wild deer. The laverock is a lark and I suppose that here, as often, the poppinguy (popinjay) is a green woodpecker, instead of a parrot. A little more explanation ought not to spoil *Nay, Ivy, Nay*, or *The Holly and the Ivy*. It is a question of men against women, when women were a subject race. Ivy, black-fruited, sober and clinging, the hiding place of screech owls was the woman's plant. Holly, armed, and growing free, with scarlet berries, had to do with hunting and the free life, it was cheerful in winter, the plant of the men. You see this in *Nay, Ivy, Nay*, a carol they sung in the fifteenth century, and much earlier, I expect, quite a pagan festival carol for the winter. I think it is explained by a custom which used to be continued in some places in England and Wales: on Boxing Day young men used to chase girls and tease them and scratch them with holly. In *The Holly and the Ivy*, the later carol we still so enjoy, the ivy has been almost pushed out, and the holly has been fitted to the story of the birth and the passion of Jesus. It would be surprising to find a full fair flock of nightingales, green woodpeckers and larks on a holly tree. But there it is: the holly has to have cheerful birds, to contradict the brown owls that everyone used to find so fatal and alarming.

THE HOLLY AND THE IVY

The holly and the ivy,
When they are both full grown,
Of all the trees that are in the wood,
The holly bears the crown:
  The rising of the sun
  And the running of the deer,
  The playing of the merry organ,
  Sweet singing in the choir.

The holly bears a blossom
As white as the lily flower,
And Mary bore sweet Jesus Christ
To be our sweet Saviour:
  The rising of the sun ...

The holly bears a berry
As red as any blood,
And Mary bore sweet Jesus Christ
To do poor sinners good:
  The rising of the sun ...

The holly bears a prickle
As sharp as any thorn,
And Mary bore sweet Jesus Christ
On Christmas Day in the morn:
  The rising of the sun ...

The holly bears a bark
As bitter as any gall,
And Mary bore sweet Jesus Christ
For to redeem us all:
  The rising of the sun ...

The holly and the ivy,
When they are both full grown,
Of all the trees that are in the wood,
The holly bears the crown:
  The rising of the sun
  And the running of the deer,
  The playing of the merry organ,
  Sweet singing in the choir.

Anon

THE WINTER BIRCH TREES

[December 1803] The two Apparition-Birch trees, close together, abreast, with the *chocolate mist* of winter branches and tresses around and above its silver body.

S. T. Coleridge

THE HOLLOW WOOD

Out in the sun the goldfinch flits
Along the thistle-tops, flits and twits
Above the hollow wood
Where birds swim like fish –
Fish that laugh and shriek –
To and fro, far below
In the pale hollow wood.

Lichen, ivy, and moss
Keep evergreen the trees
That stand half-flayed and dying,
And the dead trees on their knees
In dog's-mercury and moss:
And the bright twit of the goldfinch drops
Down there as he flits on thistle-tops.

Edward Thomas

ALL THINGS DECAY AND DIE

All things decay with Time: the Forest sees
The growth, and down-fall of her aged trees:
That timber tall, which three-score lustres stood

The proud Dictator of the state-like wood –
I mean (the sovereign of all plants) the Oak –
Droops, dies, and falls without the cleaver's stroke.

Robert Herrick

A poet I knew wrote 'We are not yet collected works, my dear.' He was, very soon. But you are not, and won't be, I hope. So I conclude this section, not with woods decaying, after all, but with these two lines by Clare. It is as if Clare was saying, All depends on me, on the continuing poem-power in myself:

O poesy, thy unexhausted powers
Gives me these summers of eternal flowers.

John Clare

4 · About birds

ALSO HE SENT FORTH A DOVE

And it came to pass at the end of forty days, that Noah opened the window of the ark which he had made: and he sent forth a raven, which went forth to and fro, until the waters were dried up from off the earth. Also he sent forth a dove from him, to see if the waters were abated from off the face of the ground; but the dove found no rest for the sole of her foot, and she returned unto him into the ark, for the waters were on the face of the whole earth: then he put forth his hand, and took her, and pulled her in unto him into the ark. And he stayed yet other seven days; and again he sent forth the dove out of the ark; and the dove came in to him in the evening; and, lo, in her mouth was an olive leaf pluckt off: so Noah knew that the waters were abated from off the earth. And he stayed yet other seven days; and sent forth the dove; which returned not again unto him any more. And it came to pass in the six hundredth and first year, in the first month, the first day of the month, the waters were dried up from off the earth: and Noah removed the covering of the ark, and looked, and, behold, the face of the ground was dry ... And Noah went forth, and his sons, and his wife, and his sons' wives with him: every beast, every creeping thing, and every fowl, and whatsoever creepeth upon the earth, after their kinds, went forth out of the ark.

From *Genesis*

THE WINTER IS PAST

My beloved spake, and said unto me, Rise up, my love, my fair one, and come away. For, lo, the winter is past, The rain is over and gone; The flowers appear on the earth; The time of the singing birds is come, And the voice of the turtle is heard in our land; The fig tree putteth forth her green figs, And the vines with the tender grape Give a good smell. Arise, my love, my fair one, and come away.

From *The Song of Solomon*

WILD DOVES ARRIVING
AND ABSORBED IN HEDGES

There is a contrast between the high flight of doves
And their douce behaviour two by two in hedges.
They fly in parties. Their wings are sharp and quick and nervy.

They have purpose. Their quick flight pauses, doves drop away
In ones for now new green of hedges, where flight from branch
To branch inside is nothing wild. Mated, their ringed
Eyes, their melody, are mild. 'Dove-grey', we say, 'dove-grey'.
At times they walk for smoothness on quiet roads.
A car approaches. Spreading white tails they rise
And are once more invisibly absorbed in hedges.

Geoffrey Grigson

WOOD-PIGEON'S NEST

I've oft been led
To climb the twig-surrounded trunk, and there
On some few bits of sticks two white eggs lie,
As left by accident all lorn and bare,
Almost without a nest; yet by and by
Two birds in golden down will leave the shells
And hiss and snap at wind-blown leaves that shake
Around their homes where green seclusion dwells.

John Clare

THE NESTING TREE-PIPIT

Where, mid the dark dog-mercury that abounds
　　Round each moss stump, the wood lark hides her nest,
The delicate blue-bell, that her home surrounds,
　　Bows its soft fragrance o'er her spotted breast,
Till startled, from the boy's rude step she flies,
Who turns the weeds away, and vainly seeks the prize.

John Clare

John Clare did not always give their right name to the birds he knew
so well (and so much better than any other English poet). His woodlarks
are always tree-pipits (which are rather similar, and used to be called
titlarks). James Fisher pointed this out. He lived in Clare's county, and
knew everything about Clare's natural history.

ST GUTHLAC'S SWALLOWS

(St Guthlac lived nearly thirteen hundred years ago, in the seventh century, and was an Anglo-Saxon hermit on Crowland, an island at that time lost in the reeds and waters of the fen country. His hermitage was the stone chamber of a barrow which had been opened and rifled for treasure: there, under a thatched roof, the saint prayed and resisted demons, according to his legend. Once he heard the demons who threw him up on their spears, talking in British – they were the Foreign Devils of the land his own countrymen had newly conquered. St Guthlac tamed birds and fishes; only jackdaws resisted his holiness.)

It happened that a certain venerable man called Wilfrith, long bound to Guthlac the man of God by ties of spiritual friendship, was talking with him in his usual way, when two swallows suddenly flew into Guthlac's dwelling, singing a song with open beak from their supple throats, showing great pleasure, as if they had reached their accustomed home. Without hesitation they alighted on the shoulders of Guthlac the man of God, went on twittering melodiously, and settled on his arms, his knees and his bosom. Wilfrith was astonished, and saying 'May I speak?', began to enquire how birds from the wild, unused to the presence of man, came to him so trustingly. St Guthlac answered, 'Have you not read that if someone be joined with God in purity of heart, all things are at one with him in God? and that whoever disdains the acquaintance of man, seeks to be acquainted with animals and to be visited by angels? Whoever is visited by men, cannot be visited by angels.' Then he picked up a little box and put some dry grass into it. As soon as the swallows saw this they began to make a nest in the box as if in obedience to a sign they already knew. About an hour later, when they had collected bits and pieces and had finished their nest, St Guthlac stood up and placed the box under the eaves of the hut where he lived. The birds began to settle down, as if they had acquired a habitation of their own. They did not presume to choose their nesting place without permission from the man of God. It was the same every year: they came to the man of God, looking to him for an indication of where they should nest. No one should think it ridiculous to look to birds for instruction in the way of obedience. Does not Solomon say, Go to the ant, thou sluggard, and consider his ways, and be wise?

From the medieval Latin of Felix, Monk of Crowland

SWALLOWS

i

The Swallow's a quick arrow, that may show
With what an instant swiftness life does flow.

Barten Holyday

ii

Out of the nostril
Of Great Buddha
A swallow flies.

After the Japanese of Issa

The Great Buddha stands in the ancient temple city of Nara, in Japan. One of the emperors set him up in A.D. 752. He is more than 50 feet high, made of bronze, much mended and venerable, but still the Universal Buddha in whom all the Buddhas are comprised.

HOUSE-MARTINS

This guest of summer,
The temple-haunting martlet, does approve,
By his lov'd mansionry, that the heavens' breath
Smells wooingly here: no jutty, frieze,
Buttress, nor coign of vantage, but this bird
Hath made his pendent bed and procreant cradle:
Where they most breed and haunt, I have observed
The air is delicate.

William Shakespeare

FOR THE NESTING HOUSE-MARTINS

June 5, 1782. My brother Thomas White nailed up several large scallop shells under the eaves of his house at South Lambeth, to see if the house-martins would build in them. These conveniences had not been fixed up half an hour before several pairs settled upon them; and expressing great complacency, began to build immediately.

Gilbert White

THE SOOTY SWALLOW

(The Swift)

Swift goes the sooty swallow o'er the heath,
Swifter than skims the cloud-rack of the skies;
As swiftly flies its shadow underneath,
And on his wing the twittering sunbeam lies,
As bright as water glitters in the eyes
Of those it passes; 'tis a pretty thing,
The ornament of meadows and clear skies,
With dingy breast and narrow pointed wing,
Its daily twittering is a song to spring.

John Clare

Clare wrote this poem in madness, which is perhaps why it seems to confuse the swift, which is sooty, with the swallow, which isn't. It is a swift all right till the last line, where swallow-like it twitters to spring, instead of screaming to the summer, like a swift.

HOW ST KEVIN MADE A BLACKBIRD'S NEST

It happened that St Kevin, deserting the company of man as he always did in the Lenten season, lived in a hut which sufficed to protect him from the sun and the rain. As was his habit he put his hand out through the window of the hut and raised it towards heaven, when a blackbird alighted and laid its eggs there in his hand as if it were a nest. Such feeling had St Kevin for this bird that he neither drew his hand back nor closed his fingers; which he held just so, without tiring, until the young ones were hatched and ready to fly. So in all Ireland St Kevin is shown with a blackbird on his outstretched hand, in memory of this wonderful event.

From the medieval Latin of Gerald of Wales

THE SHEPHERD-BOY IN MARCH HEARS
THE WILD GEESE AND THE
HERON

The shepherd-boy that hastens now and then
From hail and snow beneath his sheltering den
Of flags or file-leav'd sedges tied in sheaves

Or stubble shocks, oft as his eye perceives
Sun threads struck out wi' momentary smiles,
Wi' fancy thoughts his loneliness beguiles,
Thinking the struggling winter hourly by
As down the edges of the distant sky
The hailstorm sweeps – and while he stops to strip
The stooping hedgebriar of its lingering hip
He hears the wild geese gabble o'er his head
And pleas'd wi' fancies in his musings bred
He marks the figur'd forms in which they fly
And pausing follows wi' a wandering eye,
Likening their curious march in curves or rows
To every letter which his memory knows,
While far above the solitary crane
Swings lonely to unfrozen dykes again,
Cranking a jarring melancholy cry
Thro' the wild journey of the cheerless sky.

John Clare

THE SPOTTED FLYCATCHER

Gray on gray post, this silent little bird
Swoops on its prey – prey neither seen nor heard!
A click of bill; a flicker; and, back again!
Sighs Nature an *Alas*? Or merely, *Amen*?

Walter de la Mare

THE BLUE TIT

Bright song in May's young thorntrees.
Swift your flight bridging a hedge,
Rider of full-branched birches.
Soon-wearied wing, smooth grey bill,
You're a bird of four colours,
Green and blue, watchful servants,
White and black, tending to leaves,
Companion to young people,
Though tiny, shaper of tunes.

From the Welsh of Llywelyn Goch ap Meurig Hen

BIRD-WITTED

With innocent wide penguin eyes, three
  large fledgling mockingbirds below
the pussy-willow tree,
  stand in a row,
wings touching, feebly solemn,
till they see
    their no longer larger
    mother bringing
something which will partially
feed one of them.

Toward the high-keyed intermittent squeak
  of broken carriage springs, made by
the three similar, meek-
  coated bird's-eye
freckled forms she comes; and when
from the beak
    of one, the still living
    beetle has dropped
out, she picks it up and puts
it in again.

Standing in the shade till they have dressed
  their thickly filamented, pale
pussy-willow-surfaced
  coats, they spread tail
and wings, showing one by one,
the modest
    white stripe lengthwise on the
    tail and crosswise
underneath the wing, and the
accordion

is closed again. What delightful note
  with rapid unexpected flute
sounds leaping from the throat
  of the astute
grown bird, comes back to one from
the remote

        unenergetic sun-
        lit air before
the brood was here? How harsh
the bird's voice has become.

A piebald cat observing them,
    is slowly creeping toward the trim
trio on the tree stem.
    Unused to him
the three make room – uneasy
new problem.
        A dangling foot that missed
        its grasp, is raised
and finds the twig on which it
planned to perch. The

parent darting down, nerved by what chills
    the blood, and by hope rewarded –
of toil – since nothing fills
    squeaking unfed
mouths, wages deadly combat,
and half kills
        with bayonet beak and
        cruel wings, the
intellectual cautious-
ly creeping cat.
                        Marianne Moore

THE PHOENIX IN BRIEF

i

Th' admir'd Phoenix which admits no pair
In her perfumed ashes leaves an heir.

Francis Quarles

ii

Two sparkling eyes; upon her crown, a crest
Of starry sprigs (more splendent than the rest),
A golden down about her dainty neck,
Her breast deep purple, and a scarlet back,
Her wings and train of feathers (mixed fine)
Of orient, azure and incarnadine.

Joshua Sylvester (from the French of
Guillaume de Salluste du Bartas)

THE PHOENIX, AT LENGTH

The cubs of bears a living lump appear,
When whelped, and no determin'd figure wear.
Their mother licks 'em into shape, and gives
As much of form, as she herself receives.
The grubs from their sexangular abode
Crawl out unfinish'd, like the maggot's brood:
Trunks without limbs; till time at leisure brings
The thighs they wanted, and their tardy wings.
The bird who draws the car of Juno, vain
Of her crown'd head, and of her starry train,
And he that bears th'artillery of Jove,
The strong-pounc'd Eagle, and the billing Dove,
And all the feather'd kind, who could suppose
(But that from sight the surest sense he knows)
They from th'included yolk, not ambient white, arose?
There are who think the marrow of a man,
Which in the spine, while he was living, ran,
When dead, the pith corrupted, will become
A snake, and hiss within the hollow tomb.

All these receive their birth from other things;
But from himself the Phoenix only springs:
Self-born, begotten by the parent flame
In which he burn'd, another and the same:
Who not by corn or herbs his life sustains,
But the sweet essence of amomum drains
And watches the rich gums Arabia bears,
While yet in tender dew they drop their tears.
He (his five centuries of life fulfill'd)
His nest on oaken boughs begins to build,
Or trembling tops of palm: and first he draws
The plan with his broad bill, and crooked claws,
Nature's artificers; on this the pile
Is form'd, and rises round. Then with the spoil
Of cassia, cinnamon, and stems of nard
(For softness strew'd beneath) his funeral bed is rear'd:
Fun'ral and bridal both; and all around
The borders with corruptless myrrh are crown'd:
On this incumbent; till aetherial flame
First catches, then consumes the costly frame;
Consumes him too, as on the pile he lies;
He liv'd on odours, and in odours dies.
    An infant Phoenix from the former springs,
His father's heir, and from his tender wings
Shakes off his parent dust; his method he pursues,
And the same lease of life on the same terms renews:
When grown to manhood he begins his reign,
And with stiff pinions can his flight sustain,
He lightens of its load the tree that bore
His father's royal sepulchre before,
And his own cradle: This (with pious care)
Plac'd on his back, he cuts the buxom air,
Seeks the Sun's city, and his sacred church,
And decently lays down his burden in the porch.
    A wonder more amazing would we find?
Th' Hyaena shows it, of a double kind,
Varying the sexes in alternate years,
In one begets, and in another bears.
The thin Cameleon, fed with air, receives
The colour of the thing to which he cleaves.
    India when conquer'd, on the conqu'ring god

97

For planted vines, the sharp-ey'd Lynx bestow'd,
Whose urine shed, before it touches earth,
Congeals in air, and gives to gems their birth.
So coral soft and white in ocean's bed,
Comes harden'd up in air, and glows with red.

John Dryden (after *Ovid*)

MAGPIES

Brazen magpies, fond of clack,
　Full of insolence and pride,
Chattering on the donkey's back
　Percht, and pull'd his shaggy hide.

John Clare

WAK'D BY THE LARK

O Cresida! but that the busy day,
Wak'd by the lark, hath rous'd the ribald crows,
And dreaming night will hide our joys no longer,
I would not from thee.

William Shakespeare

The ribald crow – for crow understand jackdaw. In Shakespeare's day
they didn't bother to distinguish between rooks and jackdaws and
what we call carrion crows. Awake early, you may have heard jack-
daws chuckling round the house (perhaps they have a nest down one
of the chimneys) when everybody but themselves and yourself are
still asleep.

THE LARK IN THE SUMMER RAIN

From dark green clumps among the dripping grain
　The lark with sudden impulse starts and sings,
And mid the smoking rain
　Quivers her russet wings.

John Clare

LARK IN THE UPPER AIR

i

Like a lark to glide aloof
Under the cloud-festoonèd roof,
That with a turning of the wings
Light and darkness from him flings;
To drift in air, the circled earth
Spreading still its sunnèd girth;
To hear the sheep-bells dimly die
Till the lifted clouds were nigh,
In breezy belts of upper air
Melting into aether rare;
And when the silent height were won,
And all in lone air stood the sun,
To sing scarce heard, and singing fill
The airy empire at his will;
To hear his strain descend less loud
On to ledges of grey cloud;
And fainter, finer, trickle far
To where the listening uplands are;
To pause – then from his gurgling bill
Let the warbled sweetness rill,
And down the welkin, gushing free,
Hark the molten melody;
In fits of music till sunset
Starting the silver rivulet;
Sweetly then and of free act
To quench the fine-drawn cataract;
And in the dews beside his nest
To cool his plumy throbbing breast.

Gerard Manley Hopkins

ii

Sneezing,
I lost sight
Of the skylark.

After the Japanese of Yayū

99

iii

Resting
In the mountain pass, higher
Than the skylarks.

After the Japanese of Bashō

THE PRETTY LARK

The pretty Lark, climbing the welkin clear,
Chaunts with a cheer, *Heer peer-I neer my Dear*;
Then stooping thence (seeming her fall to rue)
Adieu (she saith) *adieu, dear Dear, adieu.*

Joshua Sylvester

THE VOICES OF BIRDS

From the woods
Came voices of the well-contented doves.
The lark could scarce get out his notes for joy,
But shook his song together as he neared
His happy home, the ground. To left and right,
The cuckoo told his name to all the hills;
The mellow ouzel fluted in the elm;
The redcap whistled; and the nightingale
Sang loud, as though he were the bird of day.

Alfred Tennyson

THE NIGHTINGALE, THE STOCK-DOVES, THE THRUSH, THE HERON AND THE WOODPECKER

The Nightingale does here make choice
To sing the trials of her voice.
Low shrubs she sits in, and adorns
With music high the squatted thorns.
But highest oaks stoop down to hear,
And listning elders prick the ear.
The thorn, lest it should hurt her, draws
Within the skin its shrunken claws.

But I have for my music found
A sadder, yet more pleasing sound:
The Stock-doves, whose fair necks are grac'd
With nuptial rings, their ensigns chaste;
Yet always, for some cause unknown,
Sad pair unto the elms they moan.
O why should such a couple mourn,
That in so equal flames do burn!

Then as I careless on the bed
Of gelid strawberries do tread,
And through the hazels thick espy
The hatching Thrastle's shining eye;
The Heron from the ash's top
The eldest of its young lets drop,
As if it stork-like did pretend
That tribute to its lord to send.

But most the Hewel's wonders are,
Who here has the holt-felster's care.
He walks still upright from the root,
Meas'ring the timber with his foot;
And all the way, to keep it clean,
Doth from the bark the wood-moths glean.
He, with his beak, examines well
Which fit to stand and which to fell.

The good he numbers up, and hacks;
As if he mark'd them with an axe.
But where he, tinkling with his beak,
Does find the hollow oak to speak,
That for his building he designs,
And through the tainted side he mines.

Andrew Marvell

A holt-fester is a woodcutter, and a hewel, as you will have guessed,
is a Green Woodpecker, which has many names: hecco, hewhole,
heyhoe, hickwall, hickward, hufil, pecker, pickatree, popinjay, rain-
bird, rainfowl, speck, speight, tree-jobber, witwall, woodhacker,
wood-knacker, woodpeck, woodpicker, woodspeck, woodspeight,

woodwall, yaffle, yaffler, yaffingale, yuckle. It is a poppinjay – which was a parrot, properly – for its bright colours, a rainbird or a rainfowl because its yaffling or yuckling, its laughing cry, was supposed to foretell rain. Some American names, to add up the score, are flicker, log-cock, and sapsucker.

MUSIC OF BIRDS

Surcharged with discontent
To Sylvane's bower I went
To ease my heavy grief-oppressed heart,
    And try what comfort winged creatures
Could yield unto my inward troubled smart,
    By modulating their delightful measures
        To my ears pleasing ever.
Of strains so sweet, sweet birds deprive us never.

The Thrush did pipe full clear,
    And eke with very merry cheer
The Linnet lifted up her pleasant voice.
    The Goldfinch chirpid and the Pie did chatter,
The Blackbird whistled and bad me rejoice,
    The Stockdove murmur'd with a solemn flatter.
        The little Daw, ka-ka he cried;
            The Hic-quaile he beside
Tickled his part in a party-coloured coat,
    The Jay did blow his hautboy gallantly.

The Wren did treble many a pretty note.
    The Woodpecker did hammer melody.
        The Kite, tiw-whiw, full oft
        Cried, soaring up aloft,
    And down again returned presently.
To whom the herald of cornutoes all sung cuckoo
Ever, whilst poor Margery cried: Who
    Did ring night's 'larum bell?
    Withal all did do well.
    O might I hear them ever.
Of strains so sweet, sweet birds deprive us never.

Then Hesperus on high
Brought cloudy night in sky,
When lo, the thicket-keeping company
Of feathered singers left their madrigals,
Sonnets and elegies, and presently
Shut them within their mossy severals,
And I came home and vow'd to love them ever.
Of strains so sweet, sweet birds deprive us never.

Anon

There the birds are some of them singing madrigals, unaccompanied, some of them playing music. The birds are a bit mixed up. Was this Elizabethan writer of songs quite sure of a difference between his woodpecker who is hammering melody, and his hic-quaile – that's to say, another hickwall, another Green Woodpecker – who is playing his part with a light touch?

It doesn't matter, because this is not natural history, it is poetry, that kind of writing, one great poet has said, in which writers combine their wish to indicate things in words with their determination to be free to use words in their own way.

In this song the cuckoo has been doing what he does in Shakespeare's song *When daisies pied and violets blue*: he has been mocking the married birds and telling them that their wives are not faithful: he is the herald of the cornutoes, the men whose wives' disloyalty makes uncomfortable horns grow on their head. Poor Margary is Madge the owl, who begins to hoot. A 'several' – all the birds, now the day is over, go off to their 'severals' – is a private property.

NIGHTINGALES, AND GLOW-WORMS

On moonlight bushes,
Whose dewy leaflets are but half disclosed,
You may perchance behold them on the twigs,
Their bright, bright eyes, their eyes both bright and full,
Glistening, while many a glow-worm in the shade
Lights up her love-torch.

S. T. Coleridge

THE NIGHTINGALE'S A CHOIR

The Nightingale's a choir, no single note:
O various pow'r of God in one small throat!

Barten Holyday

THE NIGHTINGALE SINGING

Each object to my ear and eye
Made paradise of poesy.
I heard the blackbird in the dell
Sing sweet – could I but sing as well,
I thought – until the bird in glee
Seemed pleased, and paused to answer me.
And nightingales – O I have stood
Beside the pingle★ and the wood
And o'er the old oak railing hung
To listen every note they sung,
And left boys making taws of clay
To muse and listen half the day.
The more I listened and the more
Each note seemed sweeter than before,
And aye so different was the strain
She'd scarce repeat the note again.
– 'Chew-chew Chew-chew', and higher still
'Cheer-cheer Cheer-cheer'; more loud and shrill.
'Cheer-up Cheer-up Cheer-up', and dropt
Low 'Tweet tweet tweet jug jug jug' and stopt
One moment just to drink the sound
Her music made, and then a round
Of stranger witching notes was heard
As if it was a stranger bird.
'Wew-wew wew-wew chur-chur chur-chur
Woo-it woo-it' – could this be her?
'Tee-rew Tee-rew tee-rew tee-rew
Chew-rit chew-rit' – and ever new
'Will-will Will-will grig-grig grig-grig'.
The boy stopt sudden on the brig★
To hear the 'tweet tweet tweet' so shill,★
Then 'jug jug jug' – and all was still
A minute – when a wilder strain
Made boys and woods to pause again.

                                    John Clare

★ pingle: a small enclosed field. brig: bridge. shill: shrill.

THE MUSIC OF THE MOON

As the music of the moon
Sleeps in the plain eggs of the nightingale.

Alfred Tennyson

There is a bit more to it – and there was more to it in Tennyson's feeling – than 'plain', the 'plain eggs of the nightingale'. The polished olive-brown colour, unspeckled, of the nightingale's eggs, are also the colour of some areas of a moonlit sky.

PHILOMELA

Procne, Philomela, and Itylus,
Your names are liquid, your improbable tale
Is recited in the classic numbers of the nightingale.
Ah, but our numbers are not felicitous,
It goes not liquidly for us.

Perched on a Roman ilex, and duly apostrophized,
The nightingale descanted unto Ovid;
She has even appeared to the Teutons, the swilled and gravid;
At Fontainebleau it may be the bird was gallicized;
Never was she baptized.

To England came Philomela with her pain,
Fleeing the hawk her husband; querulous ghost,
She wanders when he sits heavy on his roost,
Utters herself in the original again,
The untranslatable refrain.

Not to these shores she came! this other Thrace,
Environ barbarous to the royal Attic;
How could her delicate dirge run democratic,
Delivered in a cloudless boundless public place
To an inordinate race?

I pernoctated with the Oxford students once,
And in the quadrangles, in the cloisters, on the Cher,
Precociously knocked at antique doors ajar,
Fatuously touched the hems of the hierophants,
Sick of my dissonance.

I went out to Bagley Wood, I climbed the hill;
Even the moon had slanted off in a twinkling,
I heard the sepulchral owl and a few bells tinkling,
There was no more villainous day to unfulfil,
The diuturnity was still.

Out of the darkness where Philomela sat,
Her fairy numbers issued. What then ailed me?
My ears are called capacious but they failed me,
Her classics registered a little flat!
I rose, and venomously spat.

Philomela, Philomela, lover of song,
I am in despair if we may make us worthy,
A bantering breed sophistical and swarthy;
Unto more beautiful, persistently more young,
Thy fabulous provinces belong.

                                   John Crowe Ransom

That poet from America (where there are no nightingales) particularly mentioned hearing his bird in Bagley Wood because, I am sure, Matthew Arnold and 'The Scholar-Gipsy' were in his head: he remembered Arnold's gipsies having their tattered autumn camp (page 64) on the skirts of Bagley Wood, outside Oxford, and then lines about emerging from the forest-skirts into the moonlight and listening

with enchanted ears,
From the dark dingles, to the nightingales.

Also on the Thames, not so far from the scenes of 'The Scholar-Gipsy', Arnold one evening heard a nightingale singing among white acacia flowers. That made him write a (less good) poem about the nightingale, in England, recalling in its song what had happened to the nightingale in the Greek legends.

THE GREEN LINNET

While birds, and butterflies, and flowers,
Make all one band of paramours,
Thou, ranging up and down the bowers,
    Art sole in thy employment:
A Life, a Presence, like the Air,
Scattering thy gladness without care,
Too blest with anyone to pair;
    Thyself thy own enjoyment.

Amid yon tuft of hazel trees,
That twinkle to the gusty breeze,
Behold him perched in ecstacies,
    Yet seeming still to hover;
There! where the flutter of his wings
Upon his back and body flings
Shadows and sunny glimmerings,
    That cover him all over.

William Wordsworth

The green linnet is what we would now call the greenfinch.

THE PELICAN CHORUS

King and Queen of the Pelicans we;
No other Birds so grand we see!
None but we have feet like fins!
With lovely leathery throats and chins!
Ploffskin, Pluffskin, Pelican jee!
    We think no Birds so happy as we!
    Plumpskin, Ploshkin, Pelican jill!
    We think so then, and we thought so still!

We live on the Nile. The Nile we love.
By night we sleep on the cliffs above:
By day we fish, and at eve we stand
On long bare islands of yellow sand.
And when the sun sinks slowly down
And the great rock walls grow dark and brown

Where the purple river rolls fast and dim
And the Ivory Ibis starlike skim,
Wing to wing we dance around, –
Stamping our feet with a flumpy sound, –
Opening our mouths as Pelicans ought,
And this is the song we nightly snort; –
    Ploffskin, Pluffskin, Pelican jee, –
    We think no Birds so happy as we!
    Plumpskin, Ploshkin, Pelican jill, –
    We think so then, and we thought so still.

Last year came out our Daughter, Dell;
And all the Birds received her well.
To do her honour, a feast we made
For every bird that can swim or wade.
Herons and Gulls, and Cormorants black,
Cranes, and Flamingoes with scarlet back,
Plovers and Storks, and Geese in clouds,
Swans and Dilberry Ducks in crowds.
Thousands of Birds in woundrous flight!
They ate and drank and danced all night,
And echoing back from the rocks you heard
Multitude-echoes from Bird and Bird, –
    Ploffskin, Pluffskin, Pelican jee,
    We think no Birds so happy as we!
    Plumpskin, Ploshkin, Pelican jill,
    We think so then, and we thought so still!

Yes, they came; and among the rest,
The King of the Cranes all grandly dressed.
Such a lovely tail! Its feathers float
Between the ends of his blue dress-coat.
With pea-green trowsers all so neat,
And a delicate frill to hide his feet, –
(For though no one speaks of it, every one knows,
He has got no webs between his toes!)

As soon as he saw our Daughter Dell,
In violent love that Crane King fell, –
On seeing her waddling form so fair,
With a wreath of shrimps in her short white hair.

And before the end of the next long day,
Our Dell had given her heart away;
For the King of the Cranes had won that heart,
With a Crocodile's egg and a large fish-tart.
She vowed to marry the King of the Cranes,
Leaving the Nile for stranger plains;
And away they flew in a gathering crowd
Of endless birds in a lengthening cloud.
    Ploffskin, Pluffskin, Pelican jee,
    We think no Birds so happy as we!
    Plumpskin, Ploshkin, Pelican jill,
    We think so then, and we thought so still!

And far away in the twilight sky,
We heard them singing a lessening cry,
Farther and farther till out of sight,
And we stood alone in the silent night!
Often since, in the nights of June,
We sit on the sand and watch the moon; –
She has gone to the great Gromboolian plain,
And we probably never shall meet again!
Oft, in the long still nights of June,
We sit on the rocks and watch the moon; –
—— She dwells by the streams of the Chankly Bore,
And we probably never shall see her more.
    Ploffskin, Pluffskin, Pelican jee,
    We think no Birds so happy as we!
    Plumpskin, Ploshkin, Pelican jill,
    We think so then, and we thought so still!

Edward Lear

If it should worry you to find *The Pelican Chorus* here, there are 'real'
pelicans inside Edward Lear's imaginary ones. Edward Lear spent a
winter on the Nile, he knew its cliffs and all about the birds on its
sands and in its shallows, though the Dilberry Ducks are his own in-
vention. Or I should say they are ducks going under a name he invented.

THE CURLEW AND THE PLOVER

I never heard the loud, solitary whistle of the Curlew in the summer noon, or the wild mixing cadence of a troop of grey-plover in an autumn morning, without feeling an elevation of soul like the enthusiasm of devotion or poesy.

Robert Burns

By grey-plover I think Robert Burns means the Golden Plover, which troops and whistles in a 'wild mixing cadence'. In the letter from which this comes Burns says that he feels the same elevation when he looks at daisies, harebells, foxgloves, wild roses, birches coming into leaf, and 'hoary hawthorns', old hawthorns, that would be, covered with grey lichen and blossoming.

BLOWS THE WIND TODAY

Blows the wind today, and the sun and the rain are flying,
    Blows the wind on the moors today and now,
Where about the graves of the martyrs the whaups are crying,
    My heart remembers how!

Grey recumbent tombs of the dead in desert places,
    Standing-stones on the vacant wine-red moor,
Hills of sheep, and the howes of the silent vanished races,
    And winds, austere and pure.

Be it granted me to behold you again in dying,
    Hills of home! and to hear again the call;
Hear about the graves of the martyrs the peewees crying,
    And hear no more at all.

Robert Louis Stevenson

Whaups are curlews, peewees are peewits or plovers, howes are barrows of the prehistoric dead. This is one of the rather uncommon poems which do find words and movement – 'Hills of the sheep, and the howes of the silent vanished races' – for moorland and ancient monuments. I suppose the graves of the martyrs are graves of Highlanders killed in the Jacobite risings.

HE REPROVES THE CURLEW

O curlew, cry no more in the air,
Or only to the water in the West;
Because your crying brings to my mind
Passion-dimmed eyes and long heavy hair
That was shaken out over my breast:
There is enough evil in the crying of wind.

W. B. Yeats

Names are – or can be – in a way poems of a single word; for instance,
names of birds made from their call or song. Curlew – to me that seems
most evocative of all, evocative of time, landscape, weather. There are
plenty more – owl, chiffchaff, cuckoo, oriole, hoopoe (most delicious
and quietening monotony comes from the hoopoe), yaffle, peewit,
corncrake, crow and its Latin original *corvus*, nightjar, which is also a
jar-owl, a churn-owl, a churr-owl. And dove. And spink (for chaffinch)
and whinchat and stonechat. And America's katydid, alias bobolink
and whip-poor-will.

THE CUCKOO IN MAY

Mother o'blossoms, and ov all
That's feäir a-vield vrom Spring till Fall,
The gookoo over white-weäv'd seas
Do come to zing in thy green trees,
An' buttervlees, in giddy flight,
Do gleam the mwost by thy gay light.
Oh! when, at last, my fleshly eyes
Shall shut upon the vields an' skies,
Mid zummer's zunny days be gone,
An' winter's clouds be comèn on:
Nor mid I draw upon the e'th,
O' thy sweet air my leätest breath;
Alassen I mid want to stay.
Behine' for thee, O flow'ry Maÿ!

William Barnes

In the English of Dorset; and the third and fourth lines together quite
wonderful. When you come to it the first two times, 'mid' is 'may':
when my eyes shut, may summer be over, and winter coming on, and

may the last breath I draw on the earth not be the sweet air of the month which is the mother of blossoms. 'Mid' in the last line but one is 'might': lest (alassen) I might want to stay till May comes round. William Cowper looked at the world (page 245) and wanted to stay for ever and ever.

CUCKOO OVER THE ISLAND SEAS

A voice so thrilling ne'er was heard
In spring-time from the Cuckoo-bird
Breaking the silence of the seas
Among the farthest Hebrides.

William Wordsworth

I have heard cuckoos over the Atlantic, cuckooing invisible out of sea-mist across a sound in the Isles of Scilly (down the sound a school of dolphins was racing and jumping). Another thing is to hear cuckoo notes coming up to you to a high bare hill, like an island, which is still brown, though the cultivated land underneath is largely green.

THE CUCKOO

The cuckoo like a hawk in flight
With narrow pointed wings
Heaves o'er our heads – soon out of sight
And as she flies she sings . . .

I've watched it on an old oak tree
Sing half an hour away
Until its quick eye noticed me
And then it whewed away.
Its mouth when open shone as red
As hips upon the briar . . .

John Clare

MIDNIGHT, JUNE 30, 1879

Midnight – and joyless June gone by,
And from the deluged park
The cuckoo of a worse July
Is calling through the dark.

Alfred Tennyson

THE CUCKOO THINKS OF LEAVING

So, some tempestuous morn in early June,
  When the year's primal burst of bloom is o'er,
    Before the roses and the longest day –
When garden-walks, and all the grassy floor,
  With blossoms, red and white, of fallen May,
    And chestnut-flowers are strewn –
So have I heard the cuckoo's parting cry,
  From the wet field, through the vext garden-trees,
  Come with the volleying rain and tossing breeze:
The bloom is gone, and with the bloom go I.

Too quick despairer, wherefore wilt thou go?
  Soon will the high Midsummer pomps come on,
    Soon will the musk carnations break and swell,
Soon shall we have gold-dusted snapdragon,
  Sweet-William with its homely cottage-smell,
    And stocks in fragrant blow;
Roses that down the alleys shine afar,
  And open, jasmine-muffled lattices,
  And groups under the dreaming garden-trees,
And the full moon, and the white evening-star.

He hearkens not! light comer, he is flown!
  What matters it? next year he will return,
    And we shall have him in the sweet spring-days,
With whitening hedges, and uncrumpling fern,
  And blue-bells trembling by the forest-ways,
    And scent of hay new-mown.

                                        Matthew Arnold

P IS FOR POOL

I know a deep and lonely pool – that's where
  The great Kingfisher makes his sudden splash!
He has so many jewels in his plumes
  That all we see is one blue lightning flash.

But whether that fine bird comes there or no,
   There I'll be found before the coming night –
Beside that dark, deep pool, on whose calm breast
   Sleep a young family of pools of light.

And near my pool an ancient abbey stands,
   Where I, when lying in the longest grass,
Can see the moonlight, tender, soft and fair,
   Clasped to the rugged breast of that black nurse.
                        W. H. Davies

THE HALLOO OF THE OWL

June 13, 1802. It was a silent night. The stars were out by ones and twos, but no cuckow, no little birds, the air was not warm . . . We walked to our new view of Rydale, but it put on a sullen face. There was an owl hooting in Bainriggs. Its first halloo was so like a human shout that I was surprized, when it made its second call tremulous and lengthened out, to find the shout had come from an owl. The full moon (not quite full) was among a company of steady island clouds, and the sky bluer about it than the natural sky blue.
                        Dorothy Wordsworth

BARN OWL AND NIGHTJAR

Lovely are the curves of the white owl sweeping
   Wavy in the dusk lit by one large star.
Lone on the fir-branch, his rattle-note unvaried,
   Brooding o'er the gloom, spins the brown eve-jar.
Darker grows the valley, more and more forgetting:
   So were it with me if forgetting could be willed.
Tell the grassy hollow that holds the bubbling well-spring,
   Tell it to forget the source that keeps it filled.
                        George Meredith

He is in love, that's the source which keeps *him* filled. But this is about the one sensible stanza in a longish poem, *Love in the Valley*, which I would say is false, certainly embarrassing. Often the 'poem' inside a poem, the 'real' thing, seems to be the recreation of something seen such as the flight of the owl or the sound of the nightjar or of the spring bubbling out in the hollow.

THE BARN OWL DESCRIBES HER YOUNG

In looks my young do all excel,
Nor nightingales can sing so well.

You'd joy to see the pretty souls,
With waddling steps and frowzy polls,
Come creeping from their secret holes.

But I ne'er let them take the air,
The fortune-hunters do so stare,
And heiresses indeed they are.

This ancient yew three hundred years,
Has been possess'd by lineal heirs:
The males extinct, now all is theirs.

I hope I've done their beauties right,
Whose eyes outshine the stars by night,
Their muffs and tippets are so white.

Anne Finch, Countess of Winchelsea

From a poem in which a widow owl is making up to a lordly eagle on behalf of her daughters, like a widow in a Restoration comedy or a novel. The eagle agrees to keep his distance, in return for which widow owl will shoo off intruders in the night. One evening he comes home hungry, sees the owlets, says to himself that queer objects of that kind cannot be the daughters he has promised to protect. He'll eat them, and he does.

No more delays: as soon as spoke,
The plumes are stript, the gristles broke,
And near the feeder was to choke.

The owl comes back and wails and howls, and the lord of soaring fowls says 'Were then your progeny but owls?', telling her she has only herself to blame for telling lies about their good looks.

THE OWL

Downhill I came, hungry, and yet not starved;
Cold, yet had heat within me that was proof
Against the North wind; tired, yet so that rest
Had seemed the sweetest thing under a roof.

Then at the inn I had food, fire, and rest,
Knowing how hungry, cold, and tired was I.
All of the night quite barred out except
An owl's cry, a most melancholy cry

Shaken out long and clear upon the hill,
No merry note, nor cause of merriment,
But one telling me plain what I escaped
And others could not, that night, as in I went.

And salted was my food, and my repose,
Salted and sobered, too, by the bird's voice
Speaking for all who lay under the stars,
Soldiers and poor, unable to rejoice.

Edward Thomas

THE YOUNG BULLFINCHES

May 28, 1802. We sate in the orchard. The sky cloudy, the air sweet
and cool. The young bullfinches, in their party-coloured raiment,
bustle about among the blossoms, and poize themselves like wire-
dancers or tumblers, shaking the twigs and dashing off the blossoms.
There is yet one primrose in the orchard. The stitchwort is fading. The
wild columbines are coming into beauty, the vetches are in abundance,
blossoming and seeding.

Dorothy Wordsworth

THE SWAN

Swan, on your beautiful lake,
As white-robed as an abbot,
You are, bird, the snowdrift's glow,
Angelic hue, round-footed.
Most solemn are your movements,
Handsome you are in your youth.
God has granted you for life
Lordship of Lake Yfaddon.

Two skills keep you from drowning,
Splendid gifts granted to you:
You are a master fisher,
Look at your skill on the lake,
And you are able to fly
Far above the high hilltop,
Glancing down, noble white bird,
To survey the earth's surface,
Scanning the lake-floor below,
Harvesting shoals like snowflakes.
You ride the waves superbly
To waylay fish from the deep.
Your fishing-rod, fair creature,
Is your long and lovely neck,
Keeper of the oval lake,
Breast the colour of seafoam.
You gleam on rippling water
In a crystal-coloured shirt,
A doublet, thousand lilies,
A splendid waistcoat, you wear,
A jacket of white roses,
Withwind flowers for a gown.
You are the moon among birds,
White-cloaked, a cock of heaven.

Anon (from the medieval Welsh)

THE WILD SWANS AT COOLE

The trees are in their autumn beauty,
The woodland paths are dry,
Under the October twilight the water
Mirrors a still sky;
Upon the brimming water among the stones
Are nine-and-fifty swans.

The nineteenth autumn has come upon me
Since I first made my count;
I saw, before I had well finished,
All suddenly mount
And scatter wheeling in great broken rings
Upon their clamorous wings.

I have looked upon those brilliant creatures,
And now my heart is sore.
All's changed since I, hearing at twilight,
The first time on this shore,
The bell-beat of their wings above my head,
Trod with a lighter tread.

Unwearied still, lover by lover,
They paddle in the cold
Companionable streams or climb the air;
Their hearts have not grown old;
Passion or conquest, wander where they will,
Attend upon them still.

But now they drift on the still water,
Mysterious, beautiful;
Among what rushes will they build,
By what lake's edge or pool
Delight men's eyes when I awake some day
To find they have flown away?

W. B. Yeats

GIRLS AND SWANS

Where grey-headed withy-trees lean o'er the brook
Of grey-lighted waters, that whirl by the nook,
And only the girls and the swans are in white,
Like snow on grey moss in the midwinter's light.

William Barnes

SWANS ON THE LAKE

Now, while the solemn evening shadows sail,
On slowly-waving pinions, down the vale;
And, fronting the bright west, yon oak entwines
Its darkening boughs and leaves in stronger lines;
'Tis pleasant near the tranquil lake to stray
Where, winding on along some secret bay,
The swan uplifts his chest, and backward flings
His neck, a varying arch, between his towering wings:
The eye that marks the gliding creature sees
How graceful, pride can be, and how majestic, ease.
While tender cares and mild domestic loves
With furtive watch pursue her as she moves,
The female with a meeker charm succeeds,
And her brown little-ones around her leads,
Nibbling the water lilies as they pass,
Or playing wanton with the floating grass.
She, in a mother's care, her beauty's pride
Forgetting, calls the wearied to her side;
Alternately they mount her back, and rest
Close by her mantling wings' embraces prest.

Long may they float upon this flood serene;
Theirs be these holms untrodden, still, and green,
Where leafy shades fence off the blustering gale,
And breathes in peace the lily of the vale!
Yon isle, which feels not even the milkmaid's feet,
Yet hears her song, 'by distance made more sweet',
Yon isle conceals their home, their hut-like bower;
Green water-rushes overspread the floor;
Long grass and willows form the woven wall,
And swings above the roof the poplar tall.

Thence issuing often with unwieldy stalk,
They crush with broad black feet their flowery walk;
Or, from the neighbouring water, hear at morn
The hound, the horse's tread, and mellow horn;
Involve their serpent-necks in changeful rings,
Rolled wantonly between their slippery wings,
Or, starting up with noise and rude delight,
Force half upon the wave their cumbrous flight.

William Wordsworth

SWANS IN AUTUMN

The wild swan hurries high and noises loud,
With white neck peering to the evening cloud.

John Clare

There is another white image of flying swans, from a poem by George
Darley (he and Clare were friends), on page 204.

THE ROBIN IN THE WINTER WALK

No noise is here, or none that hinders thought.
The redbreast warbles still, but is content
With slender notes, and more than half suppress'd:
Pleas'd with his solitude, and flitting light
From spray to spray, where'er he rests he shakes
From many a twig the pendent drops of ice,
That tinkle in the wither'd leaves below,
Stillness, accompanied with sounds so soft,
Charms more than silence.

William Cowper

A ROBIN

Ghost-grey the fall of night,
  Ice-bound the lane,
Lone in the dying light
  Flits he again;
Lurking where shadows steal,
Perched in his coat of blood,
Man's homestead at his heel,
  Death-still the wood.

Odd restless child; it's dark;
  All wings are flown
But this one wizard's – hark!
  Stone clapped on stone!
Changeling and solitary,
  Secret and sharp and small,
Flits he from tree to tree,
  Calling on all.

Walter de la Mare

No, there isn't a better poem to do with the robin than Walter de la Mare's, much as there is to approve in W. H. Davies (next poem) on the robin looking, as it does, like a small hunchback in snow, or in the poem (next again) which George Daniel wrote during the Civil War. I am not forgetting, too, – but it is a line, not a poem – John Donne's description of the robin, in poetic company with 'The lyric lark, and the grave whispering Dove', as

The household bird, with the red stomacher.*

Walter de la Mare wrote his poem when he was about sixty; and maybe one does have to be getting older to find robins really alive and disturbing, instead of blobs of red on Christmas cards. They sing in a reedy way, perhaps before you are up: you hear them, then you see them flitting round, and they are 'secret and sharp and small', exactly as in the movement of Walter de la Mare's poem. The American robin bobbing in a plump cheerful way over lawns isn't at all the same.

IN THE SNOW

Hear how my friend the robin sings!
  That little hunchback in the snow,
As it comes down as fast as rain.
  The air is cold, the wind doth blow,
And still his heart can feel no pain.

---

*In *An Epithalamium on the Lady Elizabeth and Count Palatine.* A stomacher is the embroidered or coloured triangle of cloth which Elizabethan women wore down the front of their dresses and which was held on by ribbon ties.

And I, with heart as light as his,
    And to my ankles deep in snow,
Hold up a fist as cold as Death's,
    And into it I laugh and blow –
I laugh and blow my life's warm breath.

W. H. Davies

THE ROBIN

Poor bird! I do not envy thee;
Pleas'd in the gentle melody
    Of thine own song.
Let crabbed winter silence all
The winged choir, he never shall
    Chain up thy tongue:
        Poor innocent!
When I would please myself, I look on thee;
And guess some sparks of that felicity,
    That self-content.

When the bleak face of winter spreads
The earth, and violates the meads
    Of all their pride;
When sapless trees and flowers are fled,
Back to their causes, and lie dead
    To all beside:
        I see thee set,
Bidding defiance to the bitter air,
Upon a wither'd spray, by cold made bare,
    And drooping yet.

There, full in notes, to ravish all
My earth, I wonder what to call
    My dullness; when
I hear thee, pretty creature, bring
Thy better odes of praise, and sing,
    To puzzle men:
        Poor pious elf!
I am instructed by thy harmony,
To sing the time's uncertainty,
    Safe in my self.

Poor Redbreast, carol out thy lay,
And teach us mortals what to say.
   Here cease the choir
Of ayery choristers; no more
Mingle your notes; but catch a store
   From her sweet lyre;
      You are but weak,
Meer summer chanters; you have neither wing
Nor voice, in winter. Pretty Redbreast, sing
      What I would speak.

George Daniel

George Daniel hears his robin while the Civil War is being fought, and
if he does not find its singing quite as cheerful as he maintains, at any
rate it does instruct him 'To sing the time's uncertainty'. He was a
king's man, he stopped trimming his beard when King Charles was
beheaded and let it grow long and shaggy in memory of the day of the
execution in Whitehall. He never had his poems printed or published,
but they were all copied out for him in a large folio book, which was
decorated with oil paintings of himself as a young blue-eyed Yorkshire
cavalier (who should have lived in an age less troubled and troubling).
When he died Cromwell was still the Protector or dictator.

HEDGE-SPARROW'S SONG

In a quiet mood hedge-sparrows try
An inward stir of shadowed melody.

John Clare

THE PEACOCK

Mild bird, red-gold's your colour,
Fair twigs filled with marigolds.
The semblance, no ill omen,
Of a multitude of moons.
Wings of gold like a bishop,
A noble is no better hue,
Speckled and outstretched pinions,
Gold buttons on their tips.

123

Fair peacock, above the glade,
The same hue as a rainbow.
A fair sight, like coils you are,
Green dragon of church windows.

From the Welsh of Dafydd Nanmor

THE PEACOCK AND THE FIRMAMENT

Even as a Peacock, prickt with love's desire,
To woo his mistress, strowting stately by her,
Spreads round the rich pride of his pompous veil,
His azure wings, and starry-golden tail,
With rattling pinions wheeling still about,
The more to set his beauteous beauty out:
The Firmament (as feeling like above)
Displays his pomp; pranceth about his love,
Spreads his blue curtain, mixt with golden marks,
Set with gilt spangles, sown with glistring sparks,
Sprinkled with eyes, specked with tapers bright,
Powdred with stars streaming with glorious light;
T' inflame the Earth the more, with lover's grace,
To take the sweet fruit of his kind imbrace.

Joshua Sylvester (from the French of
Guillaume de Salluste du Bartas)

THE PEACOCK'S TAIL

Pride cannot see itself by mid-day light:
The Peacock's tail is furthest from his sight!

Barten Holyday

Pride, all the same, has not been the whole of our estimation of the
peacock. Peacocks had been the bird of Juno, the queen of heaven, who
watched over women and the birth of children. They were heavenly
birds, whose flesh, it was believed, never went bad. So when you see a
peacock trailing its long tail on the roof of the stable in pictures of the
baby Christ and the Three Kings and the Ox and the Ass, it is not there
for pride but as a sign of living for ever. The peacock's tail, when it was
spread, also looked like the heavens. Angels, too, were often shown
with the bright 'eye' of peacock feathers in their wings.

124

A RIDDLE

Beside the bush, behind the thorn,
I heard a stout man blow his horn.
He was booted and spurred, and stood with pride
With golden feathers by his side.
His beard was flesh, his mouth was horn,
I am sure such a man never could have been born.

(*A cock*)

COCK-CROWING

Father of lights! what sunny seed,
What glance of day hast thou confin'd
Into this bird? To all the breed
This busy ray thou hast assign'd;
     Their magnetism works all night,
     And dreams of Paradise and light.

Their eyes watch for the morning hue,
Their little grain expelling night
So shines and sings, as if it knew
The path unto the house of light.
     It seems their candle, howe'er done,
     Was tinn'd and lighted at the sun.

Henry Vaughan

COCK-CROW

I heard the homely cock by fits to crow,
With golden wings, ere dawn began to glow,
And sing his cheery sounds from high to low,
Mild in the morn, amid the glitt'ring snow;
Sweet as the nightingale, I trow, thou art.
To thy bold heart, be joy without a woe.

From the Welsh of Siôn Powel

My name it is Nell quite candid I tell,
And I lived near Cootehill I will never deny,
I had a large drake the truth for to speak,
That my grandmother left me and she going to die.
He was wholesome and sound and weighed 20 pounds
The universe around I would rove for his sake,
Bad wind to the robber be him drunk or sober,
That murdered Nell Flagherty's beautiful drake.

His neck it was green that most rare to be seen,
He was fit for a queen of the highest degree,
His body was white that would you delight,
He was plump, fat, and heavy, and brisk as a bee
The dear little fellow his legs they were yellow,
He'd fly like a swallow or dive like a hake;
But some wicked savage to grease his white cabbage
Has murdered Nell Flagherty's beautiful drake.

May his pig never grunt may his cat never hunt,
That a ghost may him haunt in the dead of the night
May his hen never lay, may his ass never bray
May his goat fly away like an old paper kite.
That the lice and the fleas may the wretch ever tease
And a biting north breeze make him tremble & shake
May a four-year-old bug make a nest in the lug,
Of th' monster that murdered Nell Flagherty's drake.

May his pipe never smoke, and his tea-pot be broke,
And to add to his joy may his kettle never boil,
May he pooly the bed to the moment he's dead.
May he always be fed on lobscouse and fish oil.
May he swell with the gout till his grinders fall out,
May he roar, bawl, and shout with a horrid tooth-ache
May his temples wear horns and all his toes corns,
The monster that murdered Nell Flagherty's drake.

May his spade never dig, may his sow never pig,
May each nit in his wig be as large as a snail,
May his door have no latch, may his house have no thatch,
May his turkey not hatch, may the rats eat his meal.
May every old fairy from Cork to Dunleary,
Dip him snug and airy into some pond or lake,
Where the eel and the trout may dine on the snout,
Of the monster that murdered Nell Flagherty's drake.

May his dog yelp and growl with hunger and cold,
May his wife always scold till his brain goes astray,
May the curse of each hag who e'er carried a bag,
Light on the wig till his beard turns grey;
May monkeys still bite him and mad apes still fight him,
And everyone slight him asleep and awake,
May weasels still gnaw him and jackdaws still claw him,
The monster that murdered Nell Flagherty's drake.

The only good news that I have to diffuse,
Is that long Peter Hughes, and blind piper M'Peak,
That big-nosed Bob Mason and buck-toothed Ned Hanson,
Each man has a grandson of my darling drake
My bird he had dozens of nephews and cousins,
And one I must get or my poor heart would break,
To keep my mind easy or else I'll go crazy,
There ends the whole tale of Nell Flagherty's drake.

Anon

THE VULTURE

Circling, circling, the vulture planes
And looks down on a desolate field.
A mother in her cabin cries,
Child, here's my nipple, feed
And grow, and though it crack
Carry the weight upon your back.

Centuries go by, hamlets
Are numbed by fighting, and by civil war,
And burn, and you're the same, my Russia,
Tragical, and lovely, as before.
How long must the mother cry
And the vulture draw circles in the sky?

March 22, 1916

From the Russian of Alexander Blok

A poem like a prophecy, because a year later began the great revolution
in Russia, the great agony blowing away the past, involving civil war
and bringing foreign troops across the country.

5 · *About beasts*

THE GALLOWS

There was a weasel lived in the sun
With all his family,
Till a keeper shot him with his gun
And hung him up on a tree,
Where he swings in the wind and rain,
In the sun and in the snow,
Without pleasure, without pain,
On the dead oak tree bough.

There was a crow who was no sleeper,
But a thief and a murderer
Till a very late hour; and this keeper
Made him one of the things that were,
To hang and flap in rain and wind
In the sun and in the snow.
There are no more sins to be sinned
On the dead oak tree bough.

There was a magpie, too,
Had a long tongue and a long tail;
He could both talk and do –
But what did that avail?
He, too, flaps in the wind and rain
Alongside weasel and crow,
Without pleasure, without pain,
On the dead oak tree bough.

And many other beasts
And birds, skin, bone, and feather,
Have been taken from their feasts
And hung up there together,
To swing and have endless leisure
In the sun and in the snow,
Without pain, without pleasure,
On the dead oak tree bough.

                                    Edward Thomas

ALL BUT BLIND

All but blind
  In his chambered hole
Gropes for worms
    The four-clawed Mole.

All but blind
  In the evening sky
The hooded Bat
  Twirls softly by.

All but blind
  In the burning day
The Barn-Owl blunders
  On her way.

And blind as are
  These three to me,
So, blind to Some-One
  I must be.

Walter de la Mare

OPEN FIELD
WHERE THE HALL ONCE STOOD

The hedgehog underneath the plantain bores,
The rabbit fondles his own harmless face,
The slow-worm creeps, and the thin weasel there
Follows the mouse, and all is open field.

Alfred Tennyson

SOLITUDE

There is a charm in solitude that cheers,
A feeling that the world knows nothing of;
A green delight the wounded mind endears
After the hustling world is broken off,
Whose whole delight was crime – at good to scoff,
Green solitude, his prison, pleasure yields,
The bitch fox heeds him not, birds seem to laugh.
He lives the Crusoe of his lonely field
Whose dark green oaks his noontide leisure shield.

John Clare

Green solitude is Clare's prison because at this time, though he could spend the day out in the fields, Clare was a patient in the asylum at Northampton, away – for ever – from his wife and his children. In another poem, which he called *Written in Prison*, he said he envied even the fly its gleams of joy in the green woods:

The fly I envy settling in the sun
On the green leaf, and wish my goal was won.

But that may have been written when he was too ill to have been allowed out.

SPORT

Hunters, hunters,
Follow the Chase.
I saw the Fox's eyes,
Not in his face
But on it, big with fright –
Haste, hunters, haste!

Say, hunters, say,
Is it a noble sport?
As rats that bite
Babies in cradles, so,
Such rats and men
Take their delight.

W. H. Davies

A SONG OF FOXES

Ho! Ho! Ho! the foxes!
Would there were more of them,
I'd give heavy gold
For a hundred score of them!

My blessing with the foxes dwell,
For that they hunt the sheep so well!

Ill fa' the sheep, a grey-faced nation,
That swept our hills with desolation!

Who made the bonnie green glens clear,
And acres scarce, and houses dear;

The grey-faced sheep, who worked our woe,
Where men no more may reap or sow,

And made us leave for their green pens
Our bonnie braes and grassy glens,

Where we were reared, and gladly grew
And lived to kin and country true;

Who bared the houses to the wind,
Where hearths were warm, and hearts were kind,

And spread the braes with wreck and ruin
The grey-faced sheep for our undoing!

And when they came were seen no more
Harrows or hoe on slope or shore,

And on the old and friendly places
New people sit with loveless faces;

And the good grey mare no more is seen
With its frisking foal on the open green,

And I seek in vain for the cow that lay
Licking its calf on the bonnie green brae!

And the bonnie milkmaids, ohon! ohon!
Are seen no more when the kine are gone!

And there's now no work for the lads to do
But to herd the sheep – some one or two!

And the goats, whose milk was good and cheap,
They too must go, to make way for the sheep!

And the roe in the rocky glade that lies
Is waked no more by the fawn when it cries,

For stags will flee, and mothers will weep
When gentlemen live to make money by sheep!

And foresters now can earn no penny
When stags are few and sheep are many.

He earns from me no kindly will
Who harms the fox upon the hill;

May he die the death of a hog
Against a fox who drives a dog!

On the hill-side may he rot
Who fires on Reynard with cruel shot!

And may the young cubs prosper well
Where snug in rocky holes they dwell

And if my prayer with Heaven prevail
No trap shall grip their bushy tail!

And may they live on tasteful food
And die as wise old foxes should!

After the Gaelic of Duncan Bàn MacIntyre

Duncan Bàn MacIntyre wasn't praising foxes for the best of reasons –
only because they ate the lambs of the grey-faced Lowland sheep
which were brought north and – with the landlords – drove the
Highlanders out of their crofts, in his lifetime. A story is told of this

poet of the eighteenth century who could not read or write. The wives and children of poets will appreciate it. He was composing poems in bed one wet morning in his heather-thatched Highland hut in Glenorchy. The rain began to drip through. 'Fair young Mary', he called out to his wife, 'Go out and thatch the roof. The rain's coming in.'

RED DEER IN THE MISTY CORRIE

In the calm bright morning when I awakened,
At the base of the crag, it was joy for me;
The grouse with her cackle, a hoarse song singing,
The courtly cock crooning brokenly;
The sprightly wren, and the musical pipe of him,
Sending the notes from him vigorous, sweet;
The starling and red-breast, with much bustle,
And cheery warble of verse most sweet . . .

The yellow-backed doe is amid the thicket
At the foot o' the saplings stripping them bare,
The buck at a courtly bed works darkly,
As he digs up the earth with bent hoof there;
The brindled kidling of barest ribsides,
With timidest nostrils, and wildest head,
Snugly it sleeps in a secret hollow
'Neath the crop o' the rush in a small round bed.

From the Gaelic of Duncan Bàn MacIntyre

FALLOW DEER AT PENSHURST

In all the woods, in all the plains
Around a lively stillness reigns;
The deer approach the secret scene,
And weave their way thro' labyrinths green.

Christopher Smart

THE BUCK IN THE SNOW

White sky over the hemlocks bowed with snow,
Saw you not at the beginning of evening the antlered buck and his doe
Standing in the apple-orchard? I saw them. I saw them suddenly go,
Tails up, with long leaps lovely and slow,
Over the stone-wall into the wood of hemlocks bowed with snow.

Now lies he here, his wild blood scalding the snow.

How strange a thing is death, bringing to his knees, bringing to his
  antlers
The buck in the snow.
How strange a thing, – a mile away by now, it may be,
Under the heavy hemlocks that as the moments pass
Shift their loads a little, letting fall a feather of snow –
Life, looking out attentive from the eyes of the doe.

Edna St Vincent Millay

THE DOES

The does
Are licking one another
This morning of frost.

After the Japanese of Issa

THE HARE IS RUNNING RACES

There was a roaring in the wind all night;
The rain came heavily and fell in floods;
But now the sun is rising calm and bright;
The birds are singing in the distant woods;
Over his own sweet voice the Stock-dove broods;
The Jay makes answer as the Magpie chatters;
And all the air is filled with pleasant noise of waters.

All things that love the sun are out of doors;
The day rejoices in the morning's birth;
The grass is bright with rain-drops; – on the moors
The hare is running races in her mirth;
And with her feet she from the plashy earth
Raises a mist; that, glittering in the sun,
Runs with her all the way, wherever she doth run.

William Wordsworth

THE HUNTED HARE

Each outcry of the hunted hare
A fibre from the brain does tear.
A skylark wounded in the wing,
A Cherubim does cease to sing,
The game cock clipp'd and arm'd for fight
Does the rising sun affright.

William Blake

ST CUTHBERT AND THE OTTERS

This circumstance is also worthy of being related, which I heard from many good persons, amongst whom was the priest Pleculf. During the time Cuthbert was with us at the monastery of Mailros, he was sent for by the holy nun and mother in Christ, Aebba. He went, therefore, according to the invitation, to the monastery called Coldingham, and remained there some days; and in nothing altering his usual habits of life, he began at night to walk along the sea-shore, singing and watching, as was his custom. He was observed by one of the brothers of the monastery, who secretly followed him at a distance, wishing to know how he passed the night. The man of God, Cuthbert, with great resolution, made his way to the sea, and entering into it, stood up to his loins in the water, whilst the waves of the sea sometimes rose to his shoulders. And when he came out of the sea, and was kneeling on the sands in prayer, two small sea animals immediately followed his footsteps, licked his feet, wiped and warmed them with their skins. After this service rendered to him, they received his blessing, and returned to their native element.

From the *Vita Sancti Cuthberti*

St Cuthbert, the saint of Durham Cathedral, is more famous for his love of the eider ducks, the 'Cuthbert ducks', whose company he shared for nine breeding seasons in the rough wilderness of the Farne Islands, where he was a hermit. About five hundred years after his death (he died on the Farne Islands in 687) pilgrims who wished to know about Cuthbert's life and about his eider ducks, could read an account of them written by one of the monks of Durham: 'These birds are particularly named after the Blessed Cuthbert . . for when he was alive he had given them in their haunts a continuity of peace and quiet, and he permitted no one to touch them, make away with them, kill them or vex them with mischievous intent. Gloriously at peace and protected by his compassion he assured these birds the same chance always of procreating their young as their parents before them had enjoyed. In fact in his lifetime, while he continued alone on the rock, he so tamed these birds to the wing and on the water that they would obey him like servants; he would tell them where they were to make their nests on the island, he would ordain the routes by which they were to come and go. So they always arrived at the appointed times, and resorting to the familiar protection of the Blessed Cuthbert they always flocked to him for refuge when they had need or were driven by adversity.'*

And the eider duck still nest there – in the first bird sanctuary.

SHEEP

When I was once in Baltimore,
   A man came up to me and cried,
'Come, I have eighteen hundred sheep,
   And we will sail on Tuesday's tide.

'If you will sail with me, young man,
   I'll pay you fifty shillings down;
These eighteen hundred sheep I take
   From Baltimore to Glasgow town.'

He paid me fifty shillings down,
   I sailed with eighteen hundred sheep;
We soon had cleared the harbour's mouth,
   We soon were in the salt sea deep.

The first night we were out at sea
   Those sheep were quiet in their mind;
The second night they cried with fear –
   They smelt no pastures in the wind.

Libellus de admirandis beati Cuthberti Virtutibus, by Reginald, Monk of Durham.

They sniffed, poor things, for their green fields,
   They cried so loud I could not sleep:
For fifty thousand shillings down
   I would not sail again with sheep.

W. H. Davies

HORSES AND HORSEMEN

Two Poems from the Japanese of Shiki

i

Summer river:
   Though there's a bridge, my horse
     Prefers the ford.

ii

   The sun's going down,
   He washes his horse
   In the autumn sea.

THE OX PUT OUT TO GRASS

Alçon hasn't led off to the red axe
Worn out by coulter and by age his hard-worked ox:
Its labour honoured, in the deep grass it now
Happily lows its freedom from the plowt

From the Greek of Adaeus the Macedonian

– Which shows that there were people kind to animals twenty-two or twenty-three centuries ago. Adaeus was a poet living in the fourth century B.C., in the time of Alexander the Great.

THE WOOD-WEASEL

emerges daintily, the skunk –
don't laugh – in sylvan black and white chipmunk
regalia. The inky thing
adaptively whited with glistening
goat fur, is wood-warden. In his
ermined well-cuttlefish-inked wool, he is

determination's totem. Out-
lawed? His sweet face and powerful feet go about
in chieftain's coat of Chilcat cloth.
He is his own protection from the moth,

noble little warrior. That
otter-skin on it, the living polecat,
smothers anything that stings. Well,
this same weasel's playful and his weasel
associates are too. Only
wood-weasels shall associate with me.

Marianne Moore

THE FLITTERMOUSE

Wonder it sees, wheresoe'er the eye doth roll:
The Bat is the air-mouse; the night's his hole.

Barten Holyday

BAT

At evening, sitting on this terrace,
When the sun from the west, beyond Pisa, beyond the mountains of
   Carrara
Departs, and the world is taken by surprise . . .

When the tired flower of Florence is in gloom beneath the glowing
Brown hills surrounding . . .

When under the arches of the Ponte Vecchio
A green light enters against stream, flush from the west,
Against the current of obscure Arno . . .

Look up, and you see things flying
Between the day and the night;
Swallows with spools of dark thread sewing the shadows together.

A circle swoop, and a quick parabola under the bridge arches
Where light pushes through;
A sudden turning upon itself of a thing in the air.
A dip to the water.

And you think:
'The swallows are flying so late!'

Swallows?

Dark air-life looping
Yet missing the pure loop . . .
A twitch, a twitter, an elastic shudder in flight
And serrated wings against the sky,
Like a glove, a black glove thrown up at the light,
And falling back.

Never swallows!
Bats!
The swallows are gone.

At a wavering instant the swallows give way to bats
By the Ponte Vecchio . . .
Changing guard.

Bats, and an uneasy creeping in one's scalp
As the bats swoop overhead!
Flying madly.

Pipistrello!
Black piper on an infinitesimal pipe.
Little lumps that fly in air and have voices indefinite, wildly vindictive;

Wings like bits of umbrella.

Bats!

Creatures that hang themselves up like an old rag, to sleep
And disgustingly upside down.
Hanging upside down like rows of disgusting old rags
And grinning in their sleep.
Bats!

In China the bat is symbol of happiness.

Not for me!

D. H. Lawrence

MOUSE'S NEST

I found a ball of grass among the hay
And progged it as I passed and went away;
And when I looked I fancied something stirred,
And turned agen and hoped to catch the bird –
When out an old mouse bolted in the wheats
With all her young ones hanging at her teats;
She looked so odd and so grotesque to me,
I ran and wondered what the thing could be,
And pushed the knapweed bunches where I stood;
Then the mouse hurried from the craking brood,
The young ones squeaked, and as I went away
She found her nest again among the hay.
The water o'er the pebbles scarce could run
And broad old cesspools glittered in the sun.

John Clare

THE CAT AND THE MOON

The cat went here and there
And the moon spun round like a top,
And the nearest kin of the moon,
The creeping cat, looked up.
Black Minnaloushe stared at the moon,
For, wander and wail as he would,
The pure cold light in the sky
Troubled his animal blood.
Minnaloushe runs in the grass
Lifting his delicate feet.
Do you dance, Minnaloushe, do you dance?
When two close kindred meet,
What better than call a dance?
Maybe the moon may learn,
Tired of that courtly fashion,
A new dance turn.
Minnaloushe creeps through the grass
From moonlit place to place,
The sacred moon overhead
Has taken a new phase.
Does Minnaloushe know that his pupils

Will pass from change to change,
And that from round to crescent,
From crescent to round they range?
Minnaloushe creeps through the grass
Alone, important and wise,
And lifts to the changing moon
His changing eyes.

W. B. Yeats

FIVE EYES

In Hans' old Mill his three black cats
Watch his bins for the thieving rats.
Whisker and claw, they crouch in the night,
Their five eyes smouldering green and bright:
Squeaks from the flour sacks, squeaks from where
The cold wind stirs on the empty stair,
Squeaking and scampering, everywhere.
Then down they pounce, now in, now out,
At whisking tail, and sniffing snout;

While lean old Hans he snores away
Till peep of light at break of day;
Then up he climbs to his creaking mill,
Out come his cats all grey with meal –
Jekkel, and Jessup, and one-eyed Jill.

Walter de la Mare

CATS AND MICE

i

Lat take a cat, and fostre him well with milk,
And tendre flesh, and make his couche of silk,
And lat him seen a mous go by the wall;
Anon he weyveth milk, and flesh, and al,
And every deyntee that is in that hous,
Swich appetyt hath he to ete a mous.

Geoffrey Chaucer

Yet can thy humble roof maintain a choir
  Of singing crickets by thy fire:
And the brisk mouse may feast herself with crumbs,
  Till that the green-ey'd kitling comes.
Then to her cabin, blest she can escape
  The sudden danger of a rape.

Robert Herrick

ENGRAVED ON THE COLLAR OF A DOG WHICH I GAVE TO HIS ROYAL HIGHNESS

I am his Highness' dog at Kew;
Pray tell me Sir, whose dog are you?

Alexander Pope

THE KING OF THE CROCODILES

PART I

'Now, Woman, why without your veil?
And wherefore do you look so pale?
And, Woman, why do you groan so sadly
And wherefore beat your bosom madly?'

'Oh! I have lost my darling boy,
In whom my soul had all its joy;
And I for sorrow have torn my veil,
And sorrow hath made my very heart pale.

'Oh, I have lost my darling child,
And that's the loss that makes me wild.
He stoop'd to the river down to drink,
And there was a Crocodile by the brink.

'He did not venture in to swim,
He only stoopt to drink at the brim;
But under the reeds the Crocodile lay
And struck with his tail and swept him away.

'Now take me in your boat, I pray,
For down the river lies my way,
And me to the Reed-Island bring,
For I will go to the Crocodile King.

'He reigns not now in Crocodilople,
Proud as the Turk at Constantinople;
No ruins of his great City remain,
The Island of Reeds is his whole domain.

'Like a Dervise there he passes his days,
Turns up his eyes, and fasts and prays;
And being grown pious and meek and mild,
He now never eats man, woman, or child.

'The King of the Crocodiles never does wrong,
He has no tail so stiff and strong,
He has no tail to strike and slay,
But he has ears to hear what I say.

'And to the King I will complain,
How my poor child was wickedly slain;
The King of the Crocodiles he is good,
And I shall have the murderer's blood.'

The man replied, 'No, Woman, no,
To the Island of Reeds I will not go;
I would not for any worldly thing
See the face of the Crocodile King.'

'Then lend me now your little boat,
And I will down the river float.
I tell thee that no worldly thing
Shall keep me from the Crocodile King.

'The King of the Crocodiles he is good,
And therefore will give me blood for blood;
Being so mighty and so just,
He can revenge me, he will, and he must.'

The Woman she leapt into the boat,
And down the river alone she did float,
And fast with the stream the boat proceeds,
And now she is come to the Island of Reeds.

The King of the Crocodiles there was seen,
He sat upon the eggs of the Queen,
And all around, a numerous rout,
The young Prince Crocodiles crawl'd about.

The Woman shook every limb with fear,
As she to the Crocodile King came near,
For never man without fear and awe
The face of his Crocodile Majesty saw.

She fell upon her bended knee,
And said, 'O King, have pity on me,
For I have lost my darling child,
And that's the loss that makes me wild.

'A Crocodile ate him for his food;
Now let me have the murderer's blood;
Let me have vengeance for my boy,
The only thing that can give me joy.

'I know that you, Sire! never do wrong,
You have no tail so stiff and strong,
You have no tail to strike and slay,
But you have ears to hear what I say.'

'You have done well,' the King replies,
And fix'd on her his little eyes;
'Good Woman, yes, you have done right,
But you have not described me quite.

'I have no tail to strike and slay,
And I have ears to hear what you say;
I have teeth, moreover, as you may see,
And I will make a meal of thee.'

PART II

Wicked the word and bootless the boast,
As cruel King Crocodile found to his cost,
And proper reward of tyrannical might,
He show'd his teeth, but he miss'd his bite.

'A meal of me!' the Woman cried,
Taking wit in her anger, and courage beside;
She took him his forelegs and hind between,
And trundled him off the eggs of the Queen.

To revenge herself then she did not fail,
He was slow in his motions for want of a tail;
But well for the Woman was it, the while,
That the Queen was gadding abroad in the Nile.

Two crocodile Princes, as they play'd on the sand,
She caught, and grasping them one in each hand,
Thrust the head of one into the throat of the other,
And made each Prince Crocodile choke his brother.

And when she had truss'd three couple this way,
She carried them off, and hasten'd away,
And plying her oars with might and main,
Cross'd the river and got to the shore again.

When the Crocodile Queen came home, she found
That her eggs were broken and scattered around,
And that six young Princes, darlings all,
Were missing, for none of them answer'd her call.

Then many a not very pleasant thing
Pass'd between her and the Crocodile King:
'Is this your care of the nest,' cried she;
'It comes of your gadding abroad,' said he.

The Queen had the better in this dispute,
And the Crocodile King found it best to be mute,
While a terrible peal in his ears she rung,
For the Queen had a tail as well as a tongue.

In woeful patience he let her rail,
Standing less in fear of her tongue than her tail.
And knowing that all the words which were spoken
Could not mend one of the eggs that were broken.

The Woman, meantime, was very well pleased;
She saved her life, and her heart was eased:
The justice she ask'd in vain for her son,
She had taken herself, and six for one.

'Mash-Allah!' her neighbours exclaim'd in delight:
She gave them a funeral supper that night,
Where they all agreed that revenge was sweet,
And young Prince Crocodiles delicate meat.

Robert Southey

THE WOLF

The rav'nouse Wolf will feed on mice and moles:
Sathan does thus devour dark earthly souls!

Barten Holyday

THE TIGER

Tiger! Tiger! burning bright
In the forests of the night,
What immortal hand or eye
Could frame thy fearful symmetry?

In what distant deeps or skies
Burnt the fire of thine eyes?
On what wings dare he aspire?
What the hand dare seize the fire?

And what shoulder, and what art,
Could twist the sinews of thy heart?
And when thy heart began to beat,
What dread hand? and what dread feet?

What the hammer? what the chain?
In what furnace was thy brain?
What the anvil? what dread grasp?
Dare its deadly terrors clasp?

When the stars threw down their spears,
And water'd heaven with their tears,
Did he smile his work to see?
Did he who made the lamb make thee?

Tiger! Tiger! burning bright
In the forests of the night,
What immortal hand or eye
Dare frame thy fearful symmetry?

William Blake

When William Blake printed *The Tiger* – setting up the type with his own hand – he picked out a y and made it Tyger; and so it usually appears. But then in 1794 tiger was spelt indifferently with a y or an i. It was often tyger in natural history books. So I don't myself think that Blake had a particular reason for printing Tyger! Tyger! He wouldn't have thought that a y was like a tiger's tail or that it made his tiger more fearful or extraordinary, or as we might say, more 'poetic'. Now that we firmly spell tiger with an i, isn't it possible that Tyger! Tyger! makes W.B.'s animal rather stuffed? At any rate, not quite so real, or burning or bright, in our imagination? When you look at a very striped tiger painted by Henri Rousseau, you don't say, 'Ah, a *Tyger*'.

THE LION AND THE UNICORN

Like as a Lion, whose imperial pow'r
    A proud rebellious Unicorn defies,
    T'avoid the rash assault and wrathful stour
    Of his fierce foe, him to a tree applies,
    And when him running in full course he spies,
    He slips aside; the while that furious beast
    His precious horn, sought of his enemies,
    Strikes in the stock, ne thence can be releast,
But to the mighty victour yields a bounteous feast.

Edmund Spenser

Many kings in the Middle Ages thought they had a unicorn's precious horn in their treasuries (mounted in gold or silver, it was usually the horn of a narwhal, a 'sea-unicorn'). They had a practical use for it. The unicorn, men believed, put his horn into water before drinking to drive away poison; so Topsell wrote in his *Historie of Foure-Footed Beastes* in 1607 that 'The horn of this beast being put upon the table of kings, and set among their junkets and banquets doth bewray the venom (if there be any such therein) by a certain sweat which cometh over it.' The lion performed the trick of acquiring this useful treasure better than a greedy jeweller mentioned in one Jacobean play★ by a character who declares he had seen, in his young travels through Armenia,

An angry unicorn in his full career
Charge with too swift a foot a jeweller
That watch'd him for the treasure of his brow;
And ere he could get shelter of a tree
Nail him with his rich antler to the earth.

In the lines by Spenser 'stour' means battle.

★*Bussy d'Ambois*, by George Chapman.

THE UNICORN

The wax-red roofings of the dawn
With pink suffuse the snowy Unicorn,
Who steps through dew-wet flowers, and eyes
The approach of hunters with a faint surprise.

They set their spears around,
He clears that avaricious circle at a bound,
He neighs, he shakes a blood-wreath'd horn,
This wounded, pure, contemptuous Unicorn.

But scenting a new presence in the trees,
He falters, turns and falls upon his knees,
And though he understands the trap,
Lays his meek head upon the Virgin's lap.

Geoffrey Grigson

KANGAROO

In the northern hemisphere
Life seems to leap at the air, or skim under the wind
Like stags on rocky ground, or pawing horses, or springy scut-tailed
    rabbits.

Or else rush horizontal to charge at the sky's horizon,
Like bulls or bisons or wild pigs.

Or slip like water slippery towards its ends,
As foxes, stoats, and wolves, and prairie dogs.

Only mice, and moles, and rats, and badgers, and beavers, and perhaps
    bears
Seem belly-plumbed to the earth's mid-navel.
Or frogs that when they leap come flop, and flop to the centre of the
    earth.

But the yellow antipodal Kangaroo, when she sits up,
Who can unseat her, like a liquid drop that is heavy, and just touches
    earth.

The downward drip
The down-urge.
So much denser than cold-blooded frogs.

Delicate mother Kangaroo
Sitting up there rabbit-wise, but huge, plumb-weighted,
And lifting her beautiful slender face, oh! so much more gently and
    finely lined than a rabbit's, or than a hare's,
Lifting her face to nibble at a round white peppermint drop, which she
    loves, sensitive mother Kangaroo.

Her sensitive, long, pure-bred face.
Her full antipodal eyes, so dark,
So big and quiet and remote, having watched so many dawns in silent
    Australia.

Her little loose hands, and drooping Victorian shoulders.
And then her great weight below the waist, her vast pale belly
With a thin young yellow little paw hanging out, and straggle of a
    long thin ear, like ribbon,
Like a funny trimming to the middle of her belly, thin little dangle of
    an immature paw, and one thin ear.

Her belly, her big haunches
And, in addition, the great muscular python-stretch of her tail.

There, she shan't have any more peppermint drops.
So she wistfully, sensitively sniffs the air, and then turns, goes off in
    slow sad leaps

On the long flat skis of her legs,
Steered and propelled by that steel-strong snake of a tail.
Stops again, half turns, inquisitive to look back.
While something stirs quickly in her belly, and a lean little face comes
    out, as from a window,
Peaked and a bit dismayed,
Only to disappear again quickly away from the sight of the world, to
    snuggle down in the warmth,
Leaving the trail of a different paw hanging out.

Still she watches with eternal, cocked wistfulness!
How full her eyes are, like the full, fathomless, shining eyes of an
    Australian black-boy
Who has been lost so many centuries on the margins of existence!

She watches with insatiable wistfulness.
Untold centuries of watching for something to come,
For a new signal from life, in that silent lost land of the South.

Where nothing bites but insects and snakes and the sun, small life.
Where no bull roared, no cow ever lowed, no stag cried, no leopard
    screeched, no lion coughed, no dog barked,
But all was silent save for parrots occasionally, in the haunted blue bush.

Wistfully watching, with wonderful liquid eyes.
And all her weight, all her blood, dripping sack-wise down towards
    the earth's centre,
And the live little-one taking in its paw at the door of her belly.

Leap then, and come down on the line that draws to the earth's deep,
    heavy centre.

D. H. Lawrence

THE WOODWOSE, OR WILD MAN
OF THE WOODS

It was to weet a wild and salvage man
    Yet was no man, but only like in shape
    And eke in stature higher by a span,
    And overgrown with hair, that could awhape
    An hardy heart, and his wide mouth did gape
    With huge great teeth, like to a tusked boar:
    For he liv'd all on ravin and on rape
    Of men and beasts; and fed on fleshly gore
The sign whereof yet stain'd his bloody lips afore.

His nether lip was not like man nor beast,
    But like a wide deep poke, down hanging low,
    In which he wont the relics of his feast,
    And cruel spoil, which he had spar'd, to stow:

And over it his huge great nose did grow,
Full dreadfully empurpled all with blood;
And down both sides two long wide ears did glow,
And raught down to his waist, when up he stood,
More great than th' ears of elephants by Indus flood.

His waist was with a wreath of ivy green
Engirt about, ne other garment wore:
For all his hair was like a garment seen;
And in his hand a tall young oak he bore,
Whose knotty snags were sharpened all afore,
And beath'd in fire for steel to be instead.
But whence he was, or of what womb ybore,
Of beasts, or of the earth, I have not read:
But certes was with milk of wolves and tigers fed.

Edmund Spenser

Caliban in *The Tempest* is really a woodwose, who knows (though you don't have to be a wild man of the woods for that) where to dig up pignuts.

Woodwoses are quite common in East Anglian churches, carved on fonts and fighting with lions. But these are good woodwoses, symbols of what happens to you when you are christened in the bowl above: they are men's souls fighting against the evils of man's nature.

Mowgli, in his way, is a descendant of the idea of the woodwose, without Caliban's nature or the nature of this 'wild and salvage man' in *The Faerie Queene*.

Some words Spenser uses are beyond guessing: 'awhape' is to terrify, 'raught' is reached, 'beath'd' is heated. Others are more obvious, 'to weet' meaning to wit, 'ravin' meaning prey, 'poke' a bag, and 'certes' certainly.

6 · *About some lesser creatures*

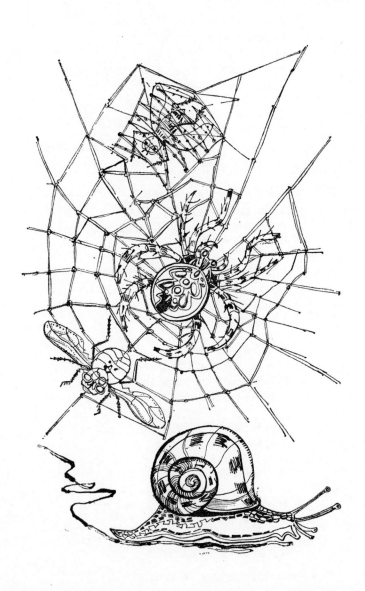

THE FROG PRINCE

I am a frog
I live under a spell
I live at the bottom
Of a green well

And here I must wait
Until a maiden places me
On her royal pillow
And kisses me
In her father's palace.

The story is familiar
Everybody knows it well
But do other enchanted people feel as nervous
As I do? The stories do not tell,

Ask if they will be happier
When the changes come
As already they are fairly happy
In a frog's doom?

I have been a frog now
For a hundred years
And in all this time
I have not shed many tears,

I am happy, I like the life,
Can swim for many a mile
(When I have hopped to the river)
And am for ever agile.

And the quietness,
Yes, I like to be quiet
I am habituated
To a quiet life,

But always when I think these thoughts
As I sit in my well
Another thought comes to me and says:
It is part of the spell

To be happy
To work up contentment
To make much of being a frog
To fear disenchantment

Says, It will be *heavenly*
To be set free,
Cries, *Heavenly* the girl who disenchants
And the royal times, *heavenly*,
And I think it will be.

Come, then, royal girl and royal times,
Come quickly,
I can be happy until you come
But I cannot be heavenly,
Only disenchanted people
Can be heavenly.

Stevie Smith

RIDDLES

Long legs and short thighs,
Rusty back and bullet eyes

(*A frog*)

I was round and small like a pearl,
Then long and slender, as brave as an earl.
Since like a hermit I lived in a cell,
And now like a rogue in the wide world I dwell.

(*A butterfly*)

Bloodless and boneless
And goes to the fell footless.

(*A snail*)

THE SNAIL

Wise emblem of our politic world,
Sage snail, within thine own self curl'd;
Instruct me softly to make haste,
Whilst these my feet go slowly fast.
    Compendious snail! thou seem'st to me
Large Euclid's strict epitome;
And in each diagram dost fling
Thee from the point unto the ring.
A figure now triangulare,
An oval now, and now a square;
And then a serpentine dost crawl,
Now a straight line, now crook'd, now all.
    Preventing rival of the day,
Th' art up and openest thy ray,
And ere the morn cradles the moon,
Th' art broke into a beauteous noon.
Then when the sun sups in the deep,
Thy silver horns ere Cynthia's peep;
And thou from thine own liquid bed,
New Phoebus, heav'st thy pleasant head . . .
Then after a sad dearth and rain,
Thou scatterest thy silver train;
And when the trees grow nak'd and old,
Thou clothest them with cloth of gold,
Which from thy bowels thou dost spin,
And draw from the rich mines within.
    Now hast thou changed thee Saint; and made
Thyself a fane that's cupola'd;
And in thy wreathed cloister thou
Walkest thine own Grey Friar too;
Strict and lock'd up, th' art hood all o'er
And ne'er eliminat'st thy door.
On salads thou dost feed severe,
And 'stead of beads thou drop'st a tear,
And when to rest each calls the bell,
Thou sleep'st within thy marble cell;
Where in dark contemplation plac'd,
The sweets of nature thou dost taste;

Who now with time thy days resolve,
And in a jelly thee dissolve
Like a shot star, which doth repair
Upward, and rarify the air.

Richard Lovelace

There is something in that poem which isn't to be expected about a
snail, on top of being an epitome of Euclid, and a moon and a sun and
a mine of gold and silver, and a saint in its own church and a friar.
Why in the last lines is it like a shooting star (which appears up in the
sky and rarifies the air) dissolving into a jelly? Because shooting stars
were supposed to dissolve into jellies; you went out in the morning,
you found star-jelly or star-shot or star-slubber on the ground dis-
solved from the night's shooting-stars. Exciting; though what you found
was really nostoc, a plant, an alga, like a bluey-green jelly, quite often
to be seen on soil or on a gravel path. A doctor who lived in Richard
Lovelace's day wrote – in 1650 – that nostoc 'understandeth the
nocturnall Pollution of some plethorial and wanton Star, or rather
excrement blown from the nostrills of some rheumatick planet.' The
strange name nostoc was invented by that strange man, Paracelsus the
alchemist.

'Point' in the poem means centre; 'ring', circumference; and
'preventing', preceding.

IN HIS SHELLY CAVE

Or as the snail, whose tender horns being hit,
Shrinks backward in his shelly cave with pain,
And there, all smother'd up, in shade doth sit,
Long after fearing to creep forth again.

William Shakespeare

UPON THE SNAIL

She goes but softly, but she goeth sure,
She stumbles not as stronger creatures do;
Her journey's shorter, so she may endure
Better than they which do much further go.

She makes no noise, but stilly seizeth on
The flower or herb appointed for her food,
The which she quietly doth feed upon,
While others range and gare but find no good.

And though she doth but very softly go,
However 'tis not fast, nor slow, but sure;
And certainly they that do travel so,
The prize they do aim at, they do procure.

John Bunyan

To 'gare' is to busy oneself.

THE RED UNDERWING MOTH

All as the moth call'd Underwing alighted,
Turning and pacing, so by slips discloses
Her sober simple coverlid underplighted
To colour as smooth and fresh as cheeks of roses,
Her showy leaves with gentle watchet foiling
Even so my thought the rose and grey disposes.

Gerard Manley Hopkins

A BRIMSTONE BUTTERFLY

The autumn sun that rose at seven
Has risen again at noon,
Where the hill makes a later heaven,
And fringing with bright rainbow hair
The boughs that lace the sky
Has wakened half a year too soon
This brimstone butterfly,
That fluttering every way at once
Searches in vain the moss and stones, –
Itself the only primrose there.

Andrew Young

WOOLLY-BEARS

i

It is a lonely life,
But hairy caterpillars fall
Round my hermitage.

After the Japanese of Onitsura

ii

The morning breeze
Ruffles the hairs
Of the caterpillar.

After the Japanese of Busōn

GNATS

As when a swarm of gnats at eventide
Out of the fens of Allan do arise,
Their murmuring small trumpets sounden wide,
Whiles in the air their clustring army flies,
That as a cloud doth seem to dim the skies;
Ne man nor beast may rest, or take repast,
For their sharp wounds, and noyous injuries,
Till the fierce northern wind with blustring blast
Doth blow them quite away, and in the ocean cast.

Edmund Spenser

Irish gnats, Irish midges – the greediest in the world, as Spenser knew (he wrote most of his poetry in Ireland, where he had his castle burnt down); midges which rise in clouds, when the wind drops, vexing everything which lives. These are the midges of the great Bog of Allen, in Co. Kildare.

LITTLE CITY

Spider, from his flaming sleep,
staggers out into the window frame;
swings out from the red den where he slept
to nest in the gnarled glass.
Fat hero, burnished cannibal
lets down a frail ladder and ties a knot,
sways down to a landing with furry grace.

By noon this corner is a bullet-colored city
and the exhausted architect
sleeps in his pale wheel,
waits without pity for a gold visitor
or coppery captive, his aerial enemies
spinning headlong down the window to the trap.

The street of string shakes now and announces
a surprised angel in the tunnel of thread,
Spider dances down his wiry heaven to taste the moth.

A little battle begins and the prison trembles.
The round spider hunches like a judge.
The wheel glistens.
But this transparent town that caves in at a breath
is paved with perfect steel.
The victim hangs by his feet, and the spider
circles invisible avenues, weaving a grave.

By evening the web is heavy with monsters,
bright constellations of wasps and bees,
breathless, surrendered.
Bronze skeletons dangle on the wires
and a thin wing flutters.
The medieval city hangs in its stars.

Spider lumbers down the web
and the city stretches with the weight of his walking.
By night we cannot see the flies' faces
and the spider, rocking.

Robert Horan

DRAGON-FLIES

i

To-day I saw the dragon-fly
Come from the wells where he did lie.

An inner impulse rent the veil
Of his old husk: from head to tail
Came out clear plates of sapphire mail.

He dried his wings: like gauze they grew;
Thro' crofts and pastures wet with dew
A living flash of light he flew.

Alfred Tennyson

ii

The dragon-flies,
All flying in the same direction,
In the rays of the setting sun.

From the Japanese of Rangai

THE GRASSHOPPER

Oh thou that swing'st upon the waving hair
    Of some well-filled oaten beard,
Drunk ev'ry night with a delicious tear
    Dropt thee from heav'n, where now th' art rear'd.

The joys of earth and air are thine intire,
    That with thy feet and wings dost hop and fly;
And when thy poppy works thou dost retire
    To thy carv'd acorn-bed to lie.

Up with the day, the sun thou welcomst then,
    Sport'st in the gilt-plats of his beams,
And all these merry days mak'st merry men,
    Thyself, and melancholy streams.

But ah the sickle! Golden ears are cropt;
    Ceres and Bacchus bid good night;
Sharp frosty fingers all your flow'rs have topt,
    And what scythes spar'd, winds shave off quite.

Poor verdant fool! and now green ice! thy joys
    Large and as lasting as thy perch of grass,
Bid us lay in 'gainst winter rain, and poise
    Their floods with an o'erflowing glass.

Richard Lovelace

THE FLEA, THE SPIDER, AND THE SILKWORM

The Flea, that feeds on dust and blood, not long
Triumphs: He's snapp'd: such is the end of wrong!

The Spider builds in palaces; her own
Is web: in th' midst whereof she's queen alone.

The Silkworm's its own wonder, without loom
It does provide itself a silken room.

Barten Holyday

FLEAS

Nat'ralists observe, a Flea
Hath smaller fleas that on him prey,
And these have smaller yet to bite 'em,
And so proceed *ad infinitum*.

Jonathan Swift

Naturalists don't observe that piece of unnatural history; but it would
seem fair if it was true. William Blake imagined – no, he saw in a day-
vision – a flea-natured kind of man. He painted this Ghost, or spirit,
of a Flea, who looks at once cruel and stupid (though can you say that
fleas are very *cruel*?). Kobayashi Issa, Blake's contemporary in Japan,
wrote more poems about fleas than any other poet. They are *his* fleas,
and he is rather kind to them, or humorous about them and himself:

I borrowed my cottage
From the fleas and mosquitoes
And slept.

THE SONG OF THE FLEA

There ruled a king long, long ago,
And he had a very fine flea,
Who could have been the king's own son,
He so adored that flea.
He called for his private tailor,
And when his tailor came
Cried, 'Measure my boy for breeches
And coats to go with the same!'

So the flea was dressed in velvets
And silks, which were of the best,
He had ribbons on his clothing,
A cross was hung on his chest.
He became a minister soon,
So he wore a star as well,
His family became very grand at court,
And that gave the courtiers hell.

Those persons of both sexes
Excessively were bitten
And the Queen and her waiting ladies
Were all abominably stricken,
And they didn't dare to scratch,
Or catch those fleas and whack 'em, –
But you and I can scratch
And we catch our fleas and crack 'em!

From the German of Johann Wolfgang von Goethe

THE FLEAS OF ST NENNAN

In Connacht there is a village well known for its church which belongs
to St Nennan. Here in old days fleas were so abundant and were such
a plague that most of the people left and the village was deserted, until,
by the prayers of St Nennan, the fleas were all driven out into a
meadow nearby.

Not a single flea thereafter could be found in the village, so filled
was it with the cleansing spirit of holiness on account of the virtues of
that saint. But the meadow has been so crowded ever since with fleas
that it cannot be entered either by man or beast.

From the Latin of Gerald of Wales

THE MOWER TO THE GLOW-WORMS

i

Ye living lamps, by whose dear light
The nightingale does sit so late,
And studying all the summer night,
Her matchless songs does meditate;

ii

Ye country comets, that portend
No war, no prince's funeral,
Shining unto no higher end
Than to presage the grasses' fall;

iii

Ye glow-worms, whose officious flame
To wandring mowers shows the way,
That in the night have lost their aim,
And after foolish fires do stray;

iv

Your courteous lights in vain you waste,
Since Juliana here is come,
For she my mind hath so displac'd
That I shall never find my home.

Andrew Marvell

THE VOICELESS WORM ON THE
UNFREQUENTED HILLS

                                    I heard,
After the hour of sunset yester even,
Sitting within doors betwixt light and dark,
A voice that stirr'd me. 'Twas a little Band,
A Quire of Redbreasts gather'd somewhere near
My threshold, Minstrels from the distant woods
And dells, sent in by Winter to bespeak
For the Old Man a welcome, to announce,
With preparation artful and benign,
Yea the most gentle music of the year,
That their rough Lord had left the surly North
And hath begun his journey. A delight,
At this unthought of greeting, unawares
Smote me, a sweetness of the coming time,
And listening, I half whispered, 'We will be
Ye heartsome Choristers, ye and I will be
Brethren, and in the hearing of bleak winds
Will chaunt together.' And, thereafter, walking

By later twilight on the hills, I saw
A Glow-worm from beneath a dusky shade
Or canopy of the yet unwithered fern,
Clear-shining, like a Hermit's taper seen
Through a thick forest; silence touch'd me here
No less than sound had done before; the Child
Of Summer, lingering, shining by itself,
The voiceless Worm on the unfrequented hills,
Seem'd sent on the same errand with the Quire
Of Winter that had warbled at my door,
And the whole year seem'd tenderness and love.

William Wordsworth

Glow-worms – you are lucky if you live where they are common –
have come to stand for love; unlike the glow-worm in Shakespeare,
which the ghost of his father mentions to Hamlet,

> The glow-worm shows the matin to be near,
> And 'gins to pale his uneffectual fire.
> Adieu, adieu! Hamlet, remember me.

You will recall lines earlier on, about the glow-worm's light and the
real eyes of real nightingales, by Coleridge (who was very familiar
with glow-worms in Devonshire, and then among the Lakes). I still
have to include one glow-worm seen by Wordsworth, the best poem
about a glow-worm that exists, I would say; though 'about' may be
wrong – it seems to illuminate Wordsworth (and his sister) more than
itself. It will come in the last part of this book, on page 243.

THE CLOGGED BUSY HUMMING BEES

The flurishes* and fragrant flowers,
Throw* Phoebus fostring heit,
Refresht with dew and silver showres,
Casts up ane odor sweit.

The clogged busie humming beis,
That never thinks to drowne,
On flowers and flurishes of treis
Collects their liquor browne.

Alexander Hume

---

*flurishes: blossoms. Throw: through

TO A BEE

1

Thou wert out betimes, thou busy, busy Bee!
As abroad I took my early way,
Before the Cow from her resting-place
Had risen up and left her trace
On the meadow, with dew so gray,
Saw I thee, thou busy, busy Bee.

2

Thou wert working late, thou busy, busy Bee!
After the fall of the Cistus flower,
When the Primrose-of-evening was ready to burst,
I heard thee last, as I saw thee first;
In the silence of the evening hour,
Heard I thee, thou busy, busy Bee.

3

Thou art a miser, thou busy, busy Bee!
Late and early at employ;
Still on thy golden stores intent,
Thy summer in heaping and hoarding is spent
What thy winter will never enjoy;
Wise lesson this for me, thou busy, busy Bee!

4

Little dost thou think, thou busy, busy Bee!
What is the end of thy toil,
When the lastest flowers of the ivy are gone,
And all thy work for the year is done,
Thy master comes for the spoil.
Woe then for thee, thou busy, busy Bee!

Robert Southey

DOR-BEETLES

The shard-borne* beetle with his drowsy hums.

William Shakespeare

---

*shard: cow-pat.

THE TRODDEN BEETLE

The sense of death is most in apprehension;
And the poor beetle that we tread upon,
In corporal sufferance finds a pang as great
As when a giant dies.

William Shakespeare

THE HORNET, THE BEETLE, AND
THE WOODPECKER

A harnet zet in a hollur tree –
A proper spiteful twoad was he;
And a merrily zung while he did zet
His stinge as shearp as a bagganet;
  'Oh, who so vine and bowld as I?
  I vears not bee, nor wapse, nor vly!'

A bittle up thuck tree did clim,
And scarnvully did look at him;
Zays he, 'Zur harnet, who give thee
A right to zet in thuck there tree?
  Vor ael you zengs so nation vine,
  I tell 'e 'tis a house o' mine!'

The harnet's conscience velt a twinge,
But grawin' bowld wi' his long stinge,
Zays he, 'Possession's the best laaw;
Zo here th' sha'sn't put a claaw!
  Be off, and leave the tree to me,
  The mixen's good enough for thee!'

Just then a yuckel, passin' by,
Was axed by them the cause to try;
'Ha! ha! I zee how 'tis!' zays he,
'They'll make a vamous munch vor me!'
  His bill was shearp, his stomach lear,
  Zo up a snapped the caddlin' pair!

Moral

All you as be to laaw inclined.
This leetle story bear in mind;

For if to laaw you ever gwo,
You'll vind they'll allus zarve 'e zo;
You'll meet the vate o' these 'ere two:
They'll take your cwoat and carcass too!

J. Y. Akerman

In the English of Wiltshire, or Wiltshire and Gloucestershire; but few
words that cannot be rightly guessed. A bagganet is a bayonet (though
hornets cannot really be described as spiteful); A mixen is a dung-heap,
lear is empty, and cadling means quarrelsome. I know people who
always say the first line, or the first two lines, of this poem when they
are driving home and cross the Wiltshire border.

THE ADDER

What, is the jay more precious than the lark,
Because his feathers are more beautiful?
Or is the adder better than the eel,
Because his painted skin contents the eye?

William Shakespeare

7 · *About rain and wind and rainbows, and still and running and falling water*

The hollow winds begin to blow,
The clouds look black, the glass is low,
The soot falls down, the spaniels sleep,
The spiders from their cobwebs creep:
Last night the sun went pale to bed,
The moon in haloes hid her head;
The boding shepherd heaves a sigh,
For, see! a rainbow spans the sky.
The walls are damp, the ditches smell,
Clos'd is the pink-eyed pimpernel.
Hark how the chairs and tables crack!
Old Betty's joints are on the rack;
Loud quack the ducks, the peacocks cry,
The distant hills are seeming nigh.
How restless are the snorting swine,
The busy flies disturb the kine;
Low o'er the grass the swallow wings,
The cricket too, how sharp he sings;
Puss on the hearth, with velvet paws,
Sits smoothing o'er her whiskered jaws.
Through the clear stream the fishes rise,
And nimbly catch the incautious flies.
The sheep were seen at early light
Cropping the meads with eager bite.
Though June, the air is cold and chill;
The mellow blackbird's voice is still.
The glow-worms, numerous and bright,
Illumed the dewy dell last night.
At dusk the squalid toad was seen,
Hopping and crawling o'er the green.
The frog has changed his yellow vest,
And in a russet coat is dressed.
The leech, disturbed, is newly risen,
Quite to the summit of his prison.
The whirling wind the dust obeys,
And in rapid eddy plays.
My dog, so altered in his taste,
Quits mutton-bones on grass to feast;
And see, yon rooks, how odd their flight!

They imitate the gliding kite,
Or seem precipitate to fall,
As if they felt the piercing ball.
'Twill surely rain, I see with sorrow,
Our jaunt must be put off to-morrow.

Edward Jenner

This Edward Jenner is the one who introduced vaccination against smallpox. Also he was one of the first naturalists to look into the secret goings-on of the cuckoo. More than these facts I think his poem tells you the kind of man he was.

NOTHING FROWN'D LIKE RAIN

I heard last May (and May is still high Spring)
The pleasant Philomel her vespers sing.
The green wood glitter'd with the golden Sun,
And all the west like silver shin'd; not one
Black cloud; no rags, nor spots did stain
The welkin's beauty; nothing frown'd like rain;
But ere night came, that scene of fine sights turn'd
To fierce dark show'rs; the air with lightnings burn'd;
The wood's sweet Syren, rudely thus oppress'd,
Gave to the storm her weak and weary breast.

Henry Vaughan

THE VOICE OF THE RAIN

And who art thou? said I to the soft-falling shower,
Which, strange to tell, gave me an answer, as here translated:
I am the Poem of Earth, said the voice of the rain,
Eternal I rise impalpable out of the land and the bottomless sea,
Upward to heaven, whence, vaguely form'd, altogether changed, and
  yet the same,
I descend to lave the drouths, atomies, dust-layers of the globe,
And all that in them without me were seeds only, latent, unborn;
And forever, by day and night, I give back life to my own origin and
  make pure and beautify it;
(For song, issuing from its birth-place, after fulfilment, wandering,
Reck'd or unreck'd, duly with love returns.)

Walt Whitman

173

THE GLITTERING STONES

March 12, 1802. The sun shone while it rained, and the stones of the walls and the pebbles on the road glittered like silver.

Dorothy Wordsworth

WHEN CROSSING A RIVER

When crossing a river in bright moonlight, I love to see the water scatter in showers of crystal under the oxen's feet.

Sei Shōnagon

Somewhere it was necessary to put Dorothy Wordsworth and Sei Shōnagon next to each other, alike and different, with eight hundred years between them. Sei Shōnagon was a lady at the emperor's court in Japan. Instead of Dorothy Wordsworth's journal in Somerset and the Lakes, she made notes – her *Pillow Book* – which she kept in the drawer of her wooden pillow. Dorothy Wordsworth wouldn't have approved of many things Sei Shōnagon thought and did and recorded – Sei Shōnagon wasn't at all a spinster. But both of them delighted in objects, in glitter, in scent, in the seasons, in snow, in water, in trees, flowers, moonlight, clouds, rain, dawn. Sei Shōnagon, too, has a perfect taste 'like an electrometer': 'Sometimes one's carriage will pass over a branch of sage-brush, which then gets caught in the wheel and is lifted up at each turn, letting the passengers breathe its delicious scent.'

THE WIND

The wind sounds like a silver wire.

Alfred Tennyson

THE SHAPES OF THE MIST

March 1, 1798. The shapes of the mist, slowly moving along, exquisitely beautiful; passing over the sheep they almost seemed to have more of life than those quiet creatures. The unseen birds singing in the mist.

Dorothy Wordsworth

MIST

Rain, do not fall
Nor rob this mist at all,
That is my only cell and abbey wall.

Wind, wait to blow
And let the thick mist grow,
That fills the rose-cup with a whiter glow.

Mist, deepen still
And the low valley fill;
You hide but taller trees, a higher hill.

Still, mist, draw close;
These gain by what they lose,
The taller trees and hill, the whiter rose.

All else begone,
And leave me here alone
To tread this mist where earth and sky are one.

Andrew Young

AN AFTERNOON SCENE

February 22. – Last night and to-day rainy and thick, till mid-afternoon, when the wind chopp'd round, the clouds swiftly drew off like curtains, the clear appear'd, and with it the fairest, grandest, most wondrous rainbow I ever saw, all complete, very vivid at its earth-ends, spreading vast effusions of illuminated haze, violet, yellow, drab-green in all directions overhead, through which the sun beam'd an indescribable utterance of color and light, so gorgeous yet so soft, such as I had never witness'd before. Then its continuance: a full hour pass'd before the last of those earth-ends disappear'd. The sky behind was all spread in translucent blue, with many little white clouds and edges. To these a sunset, filling, dominating the esthetic and soul senses, sumptuously, tenderly, full. I end this note by the pond, just light enough to see, through the evening shadows, the western reflections in its water-mirror surface, with inverted figures of trees. I hear now and then the *flup* of a pike leaping out, and rippling the water.

Walt Whitman

DURING THE LONG RAINS IN THE
FIFTH MONTH

During the long rains in the Fifth Month, there is something very moving about a place with a pond. Between the dense irises, water-oats, and other plants one can see the green of the water; and the centre garden seems to be the same green colour. One stays there all day long, gazing in contemplation at the clouded sky – oh, how moving it is!

I am always moved and delighted by places that have ponds – not only in the winter (when I love waking up to find that the water has frozen over) but at every time of the year. The ponds I like best are not those in which everything is carefully laid out; I much prefer one that has been left to itself so that it is wild and covered with weeds. At night in the green spaces of water one can see nothing but the pale glow of the moonlight. At any time and in any place I find moonlight very moving.

Sei Shōnagon

THE RAINBOW

Still young and fine! but what is still in view
We slight as old and soil'd, though fresh and new.
How bright wert thou, when Shem's admiring eye
Thy burnish'd, flaming arch did first descry!
When Terah, Nahor, Haran, Abram, Lot,
The youthful world's gray fathers in one knot,
Did with intentive looks watch every hour
For thy new light, and trembled at each shower!
When thou dost shine, Darkness looks white and fair,
Forms turn to Music, clouds to smiles and air:
Rain gently spends his honey-drops, and pours
Balm on the cleft earth, milk on grass and flowers.

Henry Vaughan

'When thou dost shine, Darkness looks white and fair' – here is a chance of saying one thing about Vaughan, who was Welsh, and lived in the Vale of Usk – *Olor Iscanus*, the Swan of Usk – in view of the Black Mountains, which are blue by day, and black when the sun drops behind them. He loved the word 'white'. His biographer* says

---

*F. E. Hutchinson, in *Henry Vaughan*.

that white was Vaughan's adjective 'for all he valued most', and that it showed his Welshness, since *gwyn*, white, signifies in Welsh 'not only white but fair, happy, holy, blessed . . . a Welsh word for Paradise is *gwynfyd*, the white world.' He used white, in one poem, of the books in the Bodleian Library at Oxford, since books were

> Burning and shining thoughts; man's posthume day:
> The track of fled souls, and their Milky Way.
> The dead alive and busy, the still voice
> Of inlarg'd spirits, kind heav'n's white decoys.

His other favourite is 'green', as in the lines about rain some pages back.

COLOURS OF THE RAINBOW

> When the rainbow arching high
> Looks from the zenith round the sky,
> Lit with exquisite tints seven
> Caught from angels' wings in heaven.
>
> *Gerard Manley Hopkins*

Hopkins gives the rainbow seven tints, old Archdeacon Holyday, in the next lines, gives it three colours, red, green and blue. Really of course there are six colours, three primary, three mixed between the primaries, red, orange, yellow, green, blue and violet – though they may not all be visible. Our ancestors gave the rainbow seven colours so that it would fit into the long list of things which divided into sacred sevens, Seven Heavens, Seven Planets, Seven Days of creation, Seven Ages of Man, Seven Deadly Sins, Seven Sacraments, and so on. We go on talking about the rainbow in the same way – I mean taking the seven colours for granted. When I wrote this I asked a scientist, an artist and a writer and someone home from school, How many colours are there in the rainbow? They all said seven, they would not believe it was six. One of them knew the memory sentence giving the colours in their right order from outside to inside of the bow, *Richard of York gained battles in vain*, and said 'There you are, in for indigo, which makes seven'. But though the colours merge into each other, indigo between blue and violet is really cheating. Leave out the 'in': *Richard of York gained battles vainly.* And remember what I wrote at the very beginning: poetry to do with nature isn't natural history.

THE RAINBOW'S DECLARATION

By red, green, blue, which sometimes paint the air,
Guilt, Pardon, Heav'n, the Rainbow does declare.

Barten Holyday

A GREAT TIME

Sweet Chance, that led my steps abroad,
   Beyond the town, where wild flowers grow –
A rainbow and a cuckoo, Lord,
   How rich and great the times are now!
     Know, all ye sheep
     And cows, that keep

On staring that I stand so long
   In grass that's wet from heavy rain –
A rainbow and a cuckoo's song
   May never come together again;
     May never come
     This side the tomb.

W. H. Davies

ENTRY OF WELCOME

The rainbow bends me an entry of welcome
Over the way I am going
Into the width of the houses and cloud. And behind
Me the sun, coming warm on my neck,

Freshens all for my eyes. O the elm trunks
Quickly are green, O brilliant the bullfinch,
Vivid the field; and there by one foot
Of the bow

The birds glitter white, white
As they turn, on the purple of clouds. And new
Are the roofs, are red, to me going
Into the difficult dark through
The gateway of colours.

Geoffrey Grigson

THE SHOWER

Waters above! eternal Springs!
The dew, that silvers the Dove's wings!
O welcome, welcome to the sad:
Give dry dust drink, drink that makes glad!
Many fair ev'nings, many flow'rs
Sweeten'd with rich and gentle showers,
Have I enjoy'd, and down have run
Many a fine and shining sun;
But never, till this happy hour,
Was blest with such an evening-shower!

Henry Vaughan

There is a wide sleepy lake, Llangorse Pool, near Henry Vaughan's
home in Wales. He wrote another poem also called *The Shower*, which
begins with the shower's birth, as he thought, in the vapour breathed
up by the lake:

'Twas so, I saw thy birth: That drowsy Lake
From her faint bosom breath'd thee, the disease
Of her sick waters, and infectious ease.
    But, now at even
    Too gross for heaven,
Thou fall'st in tears, and weep'st for thy mistake.

That is exactly how the lake appears, on some days, drowsy with a
faint bosom.

THE COLD SPRING

Traveller, don't drink the sun-warmed water
Of this beck my trailing sheep have muddied so,
But climb the hill there where the heifers graze,
Go on a yard or two, and you will find below
That shepherds' pine, bubbling from wet rock,
A spring colder than northern snow.

From the Greek of Leonidas

EASTWELL

No more I rambled to the pasture brook,
Where in my youth, at Eastwell's fountain side,
Which winter never froze nor summer dried,
Young men and maidens used to talk and play
In the cool shadow of its willows grey,
Drinking love healths in mugs of sugar'd drink
On the soft swellings of its rushy brink,
By the spring head whose water, winter-chill,
Boils up the white sand that is never still,
Now swimming up in silver threads, and then
Slow siling down to bubble up agen.

John Clare

'Siling' is sliding or gliding. Often such springs have a still surface, are still almost to the bottom, where only the movement of sand, bubbling up and siling back, reveals the birth of water.

THE STREAM TO THE OCEAN

The current that with gentle murmur glides,
Thou know'st, being stopp'd, impatiently doth rage;
But when his fair course is not hindered,
He makes sweet music with the enamell'd stones,
Giving a gentle kiss to every sedge
He overtaketh in his pilgrimage;
And so by many winding nooks he strays
With willing sport to the wild ocean.
Then let me go, and hinder not my course.
I'll be as patient as a gentle stream,
And make a pastime of each weary step,
Till the last step have brought me to my love;
And there I'll rest, as after much turmoil
A blessed soul doth in Elysium.

William Shakespeare

I HEAR A RIVER

I hear a river thro' the valley wander
Whose water runs, the song alone remaining.
A rainbow stands and summer passes under.

Trumbull Stickney

THE OLD SUMMERHOUSE

This blue-washed, old, thatched summerhouse –
Paint scaling, and fading from its walls –
How often from its hingeless door
I have watched – dead leaf, like the ghost of a mouse,
Rasping the worn brick floor –
The snows of the weir descending below,
And their thunderous waterfall.

Fall – fall: dark, garrulous rumour,
Until I could listen no more.
Could listen no more – for beauty with sorrow
Is a burden hard to be borne;
The evening light on the foam, and the swans, there;
That music, remote, forlorn.

Walter de la Mare

THERE BY THE WEST-MIRRORED OSIERS

See, on the river the slow-rippled surface,
Shining; the slow ripple broadens in circles; the bright surface smoothens;
Now it is flat as the leaves of the yet unseen water-lily.
There dart the lives of a day, ever-varying tactics fantastic.
There by the wet-mirrored osiers, the emerald wing of the kingfisher
Flashes, the fish in his beak! there the dab-chick dived, and the motion
Lazily undulates all thro' the tall standing army of rushes.

George Meredith

BLUE FISHES IN THE CRYSTAL STREAM

Lytill fischis by the brim,
Now here, now there, with backis blue as lead,
Lap and playit, and in a rout gan swim
So prattily, and dressit tham to spread
Their coral finnis, as the ruby red,
That in the sonne on their scalis bright
As gesserant aye glitterit in my sight.

King James I of Scotland

'Real' fishes? King James *could* have meant roach, I suppose even trout. But he wasn't writing a handbook of fishes. Lap is leapt; and gesserant, jesserant, is a word taken from the Saracens, it means coat armour made up of bright splints of steel.

RISING TROUT

June 8, 1802. The trout leaping in the sunshine spreads on the bottom of the river concentric circles of light.

S. T. Coleridge

THE TARN

The Boy from his bedroom window
Looked over the little town,
And away to the bleak black upland
Under a clouded moon.

The moon came forth from her cavern;
He saw the sudden gleam
Of a tarn in the swarthy moorland;
Or perhaps the whole was a dream.

For I never could find that water
In all my walks and rides:
Far-off in the Land of Memory
That midnight pool abides.

Many fine things had I a glimpse of
    And said 'I shall find them one day.'
Whether within or without me
    They were, I cannot say.

               William Allingham

An Irish poet (though he gave up Ireland for London and Hampshire),
and you must think of an Irish tarn among the mountains and in the
swarthy moorland of Donegal, where he grew up.

THERE WAS A BOY

There was a Boy; ye knew him well, ye cliffs
And islands of Winander! – many a time,
At evening, when the earliest stars began
To move along the edges of the hills,
Rising or setting, would he stand alone,
Beneath the trees, or by the glimmering lake;
And there, with fingers interwoven, both hands
Pressed closely palm to palm and to his mouth
Uplifted, he, as through an instrument,
Blew mimic hootings to the silent owls,
That they might answer him. – And they would shout
Across the water vale, and shout again,
Responsive to his call, – with quivering peals,
And long halloos, and screams, and echoes loud
Redoubled and redoubled; concourse wild
Of jocund din! And, when there came a pause
Of silence such as baffled his best skill:
Then sometimes, in that silence, while he hung
Listening, a gentle shock of mild surprise
Has carried far into his heart the voice
Of mountain-torrents; or the visible scene
Would enter unawares into his mind
With all its solemn imagery, its rocks,
Its woods, and that uncertain heaven received
Into the bosom of the steady lake.

    This boy was taken from his mates, and died
In childhood, ere he was full twelve years old.
Pre-eminent in beauty is the vale;

Where he was born and bred: the churchyard hangs
Upon a slope above the village-school;
And through that churchyard when my way has led
On summer-evenings, I believe that there
A long half-hour together I have stood
Mute – looking at the grave in which he lies!

William Wordsworth

EVENING ON CALM LAKES

Sweet are the sounds that mingle from afar,
Heard by calm lakes, as peeps the folding star,
Where the duck dabbles 'mid the rustling sedge,
And feeding pike starts from the water's edge,
Or the swan stirs the reeds, his neck and bill
Wetting, that drip upon the water still;
And heron, as resounds the trodden shore,
Shoots upward, darting his long neck before.

William Wordsworth

Did English shepherds, or shepherds in the Lake District, call the Evening Star the 'folding star'? I don't know. The Greek shepherds did, or at any rate Greek poets, as English poets would have known. The coming into sight of the Evening Star told shepherds when their flocks should be folded for the night. The poet Callimachus wrote more than thirteen hundred years ago of

The star of the fold
Which goes to its setting with the sun.

(To be fair he may have written that it sets, as it does, 'after the sun'.)

A MORTAL IS DEAD

Raised are the dripping oars,
Silent the boat! the lake,
Lovely and soft as a dream,
Swims in the sheen of the moon.
The mountains stand at its head
Clear in the pure June-night,

But the valleys are flooded with haze.
Rydal and Fairfield are there;
In the shadow Wordsworth lies dead.
So it is, so it will be for aye.
Nature is fresh as of old,
Is lovely; a mortal is dead.

Matthew Arnold

THE SEVERN AND THE WYE

There twice a day the Severn fills;
   The salt sea-water passes by,
   And hushes half the babbling Wye,
And makes a silence in the hills.

Alfred Tennyson

FRATER AVE ATQUE VALE

Row us out from Desenzano, to your Sirmione row!
So they rowed, and there we landed – 'O venusta Sirmio!'
There to me through all the groves of olive in the summer glow,
There beneath the Roman ruin where the purple flowers grow,
Came that 'Ave atque Vale' of the Poet's hopeless woe,
Tenderest of Roman poets nineteen-hundred years ago,
'Frater Ave atque Vale' – as we wandered to and fro
Gazing at the Lydian laughter of the Garda Lake below
Sweet Catullus's all-but-island, olive-silvery Sirmio!

Alfred Tennyson

This needs a little explaining. Catullus, the Roman poet, wrote one poem about 'lovely Sirmio', the peninsula at the end of Lake Garda below the Alps; and he wrote another poem, when his brother died, ending '*frater, ave atque vale*', 'brother, welcome and goodbye'. Tennyson remembered both these poems when he was rowed over the lake to Sirmio (which the Italians call Sirmione) after his own brother's death. At the end of the peninsula there are no houses, there are still olive trees, you can see the small waves seeming to laugh on the shallow rocks below, as Catullus describes them, and Tennyson. You can look across the lake to the mountains, seeing what these two poets saw, and you can feel that the writing of poems goes on for ever.

INVERSNAID

This darksome burn, horseback brown,
His rollrock highroad roaring down,
In coop and in comb the fleece of his foam
Flutes and low to the lake falls home.

A windpuff-bonnet of fáwn-fróth
Turns and twindles over the broth
Of a pool so pitchblack, féll-frówning,
It rounds and rounds Despair to drowning.

Degged with dew, dappled with dew
Are the groins of the braes that the brook treads through,
Wiry heathpacks, flitches of fern,
And the beadbonny ash that sits over the burn.

What would the world be, once bereft
Of wet and of wildness? Let them be left,
O let them be left, wildness and wet;
Long live the weeds and the wilderness yet.

Gerard Manley Hopkins

BREEZE FROM THE WATERFALL

Two crescent hills
Fold in behind each other, and so make
A circular vale, and land-locked, as might seem,
With brook and bridge, and grey stone cottages,
Half hid by rocks and fruit-trees. At my feet,
The whortle-berries are bedewed with spray,
Dashed upwards by the furious waterfall.
How solemnly the pendent ivy-mass
Swings in its winnow: All the air is calm.
The smoke from cottage-chimneys, tinged with light,
Rises in columns; from this house alone,
Close by the waterfall, the column slants,
And feels its ceaseless breeze.

S. T. Coleridge

A WATERFALL

Full-faced above the valley stood the moon;
And like a downward smoke, the slender stream
Along the cliff to fall and pause and fall did seem.

Alfred Tennyson

LISTENING TO THE WATERFALLS

i

April 29, 1802. A beautiful morning – the sun shone and all was pleasant. . . . William lay, and I lay, in the trench under the fence – he with his eyes shut, and listening to the waterfalls and the birds. There was no one waterfall above another – it was a sound of waters in the air – the voice of the air. William heard me breathing and rustling now and then, but we both lay still, and unseen by one another; he thought that it would be as sweet thus to lie so in the grave, to hear the *peaceful* sounds of the earth, and just to know that our dear friends were near.

Dorothy Wordsworth

ii

A cold night!
The sound of a waterfall
Falling into the sea.

After the Japanese of Kyokusui

THE MOUNTAIN

The burn ran blacker for the snow
And ice-floe on ice-floe
Jangled in heavy lurches
Beneath the claret-coloured birches.

Dark grouse rose becking from the ground
And deer turned sharp heads round,
The antlers on their brows
Like stunted trees with withered boughs.

I climbed to where the mountain sloped
And long wan bubbles groped
Under the ice's cover,
A bridge that groaned as I crossed over.

I reached the mist, brighter than day,
That showed a specious way
By narrow crumbling shelves,
Where rocks grew larger than themselves.

But when I saw the mountain's spire
Looming through that damp fire,
I left it still unwon
And climbed down to the setting sun.

Andrew Young

8 · *About beaches, sea, waves and sea creatures*

THE PEACOCK SEA

June 8, 1848. Walked seaward. Large crimson clover; sea purple and green like a peacock's neck. 'By bays, the peacock's neck in hue.'

Alfred Tennyson

THE HERMIT

Delightful I think it to be in the bosom of an isle
on the crest of a rock,
that I may look there on the manifold
face of the sea.

That I may see its heavy waves
over the glittering ocean
as they chant a melody to their Father
on their eternal course.

That I may see its smooth strand of clear headlands,
no gloomy thing;
that I may hear the voice of the wondrous birds,
a joyful course.

That I may hear the sound of the shallow waves
against the rocks;
that I may hear the cry beside the churchyard,
the roar of the sea.

That I may see its splendid flocks of birds
over the full-watered ocean;
that I may see its mighty whales,
greatest of wonders.

That I may see its ebb and its flood-tide
in its flow;
that this should be my name, a secret I declare,
'He who turned his back on Ireland.'

That contrition of heart should come upon me
when I look on it;
that I may bewail my many sins
difficult to declare.

That I may bless the Lord
who has power over all
heaven with its crystal orders of angels,
earth, ebb, flood tide.

That I may pore on one of my books,
good for my soul,
a while kneeling for beloved heaven,
a while at psalms.

A while meditating upon the Prince of Heaven,
holy is the redemption,
a while at labour not too heavy;
it would be delightful!

A while gathering dilisk from the rock,
a while fishing,
a while giving food to the poor,
a while in my cell.

The counsel which is best before God
may He confirm it to me,
may the King, whose servant I am, not desert me,
may He not deceive me.

Anon (from the medieval Irish)

THE SUMMER SEA

The moon is setting;
The morning tide flows fast;
The summer sea.

After the Japanese of Sōgi

NEITHER OUT FAR NOR IN DEEP

The people along the sand
All turn and look one way.
They turn their back on the land.
They look at the sea all day.

191

As long as it takes to pass
A ship keeps raising its hull;
The wetter ground like glass
Reflects a standing gull.

The land may vary more;
But wherever the truth may be –
The water comes ashore,
And the people look at the sea.

They cannot look out far.
They cannot look in deep.
But when was that ever a bar
To any watch they keep?

Robert Frost

ON THE SANDS OF PAUMANOK'S SHORE:
THE SEA OF WALT WHITMAN

Throwing myself on the sand, confronting the waves,
I, chanter of pains and joys, uniter of here and hereafter,
Taking all hints to use them, but swiftly leaping beyond them,
A reminiscence sing.

Once Paumanok,
When the lilac-scent was in the air and Fifth-month grass was growing,
Up this seashore in some briers,
Two feather'd guests from Alabama, two together,
And their nest, and four light-green eggs spotted with brown,
And every day the he-bird to and fro near at hand,
And every day the she-bird crouch'd on her nest, silent, with bright
    eyes,
And every day I, a curious boy, never too close, never disturbing them,
Cautiously peering, absorbing, translating.

Shine! shine! shine!
Pour down your warmth, great sun!
While we bask, we two together.

Two together!
Winds blow south, or winds blow north,
Day come white, or night come black,
Home, or rivers and mountains from home,
Singing all time, minding no time,
While we two keep together.

Till of a sudden,
May-be kill'd, unknown to her mate,
One forenoon the she-bird crouch'd not on the nest,
Nor return'd that afternoon, nor the next,
Nor ever appear'd again.

And thenceforward all summer in the sound of the sea,
And at night under the full of the moon in calmer weather,
Over the hoarse surging of the sea,
Or flitting from brier to brier by day,
I saw, I heard at intervals the remaining one, the he-bird,
The solitary guest from Alabama.

Blow! blow! blow!
Blow up sea-winds along Paumanok's shore;
I wait and I wait till you blow my mate to me.

Yes, when the stars glisten'd,
All night long on the prong of a moss-scallop'd stake,
Down almost amid the slapping waves,
Sat the lone singer wonderful causing tears.

He call'd on his mate,
He pour'd forth the meanings which I of all men know.

Yes my brother I know,
The rest might not, but I have treasur'd every note,
For more than once dimly down to the beach gliding,
Silent, avoiding the moonbeams, blending myself with the shadows,
Recalling now the obscure shapes, the echoes, the sounds and sights
    after their sorts.
The white arms out in the breakers tirelessly tossing,
I, with bare feet, a child, the wind wafting my hair,
Listen'd long and long.

Listen'd to keep, to sing, now translating the notes,
Following you my brother.

Soothe! soothe! soothe!
Close on its wave soothes the wave behind,
And again another behind embracing and lapping, every one close,
But my love soothes not me, not me.

Low hangs the moon, it rose late,
It is lagging – O I think it is heavy with love, with love.

O madly the sea pushes upon the land,
With love, with love.

O night! do I not see my love fluttering out among the breakers?
What is that little black thing I see there in the white?

Loud! loud! loud!
Loud I call to you, my love!
High and clear I shoot my voice over the waves,
Surely you must know who is here, is here,
You must know who I am, my love.

Low-hanging moon!
What is that dusky spot in your brown yellow?
O it is the shape, the shape of my mate!
O moon do not keep her from me any longer.

Land! land! O land!
Whichever way I turn, O I think you could give me my mate back again if
* you only would,*
For I am almost sure I see her dimly whichever way I look.

O rising stars!
Perhaps the one I want so much will rise, will rise with some of you.

O throat! O trembling throat!
Sound clearer through the atmosphere!
Pierce the woods, the earth,
Somewhere listening to catch you must be the one I want.

Walt Whitman

Paumanok was the Indian name for Long Island. Walt Whitman was born on Long Island, before it was the home of millions of commuters. It was covered with cattle, wearing bells, and with horses. Whitman learnt the sea and the shore on its endless, empty beaches. He made friends with the herdsmen and fishermen, collected gull's eggs, dug up clams, speared plump eels through holes cut in the ice of the frozen shallows. He watched the roll of the Atlantic, he remembered always the loneliness, the smell of sea and the shore, and the feel of the sand on his naked feet. Later on at the New York end of his Paumanok, at Coney Island, when it was still 'a long, bare unfrequented shore', which he had to himself, he would bathe and then 'race up and down the hard sand and declaim Homer or Shakespeare to the surf and the sea-gulls by the hour.' That is why he came to write his sea poems.

A PAUMANOK PICTURE

Two boats with nets lying off the sea-beach, quite still,
Ten fishermen waiting – they discover a thick school of mossbonkers
    – they drop the join'd seine-ends in the water,
The boats separate and row off, each on its rounding course to the
    beach, enclosing the mossbonkers,
The net is drawn in by a windlass by those who stop ashore,
Some of the fishermen lounge in their boats, others stand ankle-deep
    in the water, pois'd on strong legs,
The boats partly drawn up, the water slapping against them,
Strew'd on the sand in heaps and windrows, well out from the water,
    the green-back'd spotted mossbonkers.

Walt Whitman

LINCOLNSHIRE SEA (AT MABLETHORPE)

Here often, when a child, I lay reclined,
I took delight in this locality.
Here stood the infant Ilion of the mind,
And here the Grecian ships did seem to be.
And here again I come, and only find
The drain-cut levels of the marshy lea, –
Gray sandbanks, and pale sunsets, – dreary wind,
Dim shores, dense rains, and heavy-clouded sea!

Alfred Tennyson

This and the two sea-pictures which follow are Tennyson's special sea, which he knew when he was a boy. Paumanok for Whitman, for Tennyson the Lincolnshire beaches at Mablethorpe (now something of a Coney Island in summer) sliding into the North Sea. He knew these beaches day, night, and dawn, winter and summer (once he met a fisherman on the Mablethorpe shore at 4 a.m. on a summer morning. When he said 'Good-day' the fisherman replied 'Thou poor fool, thou doesn't know whether it be day or night'). Tennyson liked to stand on the line of sand-dunes at Mablethorpe: if he looked one way, there was the North Sea, calm or wild, if he looked the other way, there were the flat marshes. 'I used to stand on this sand-built ridge, and think that it was the spine-bone of the world.' When he had poems to finish, or newly published books to celebrate, Tennyson liked to come back to Mablethorpe.

'At night on the shore, when the tide is full, the sound is amazing. All around there is a low murmur of seething foam . . . Nowhere have the breakers a more thunderous roar than on this Lincolnshire coast; and sometimes at half-tide the clap of the wave falling on the flat shore can be heard for miles.'*

---

*Tennyson's son Hallam, in *Alfred Lord Tennyson: A Memoir*.

A SLOW-ARCHING WAVE

As the crest of some slow-arching wave,
Heard in dead night along that table-shore,
Drops flat, and after the great waters break
Whitening for half a league, and thin themselves,
Far over sands marbled with moon and cloud,
From less and less to nothing.

Alfred Tennyson

A POOL UPON THE SANDS

A still salt pool, locked in with bars of sand,
   Left on the shore; that hears all night
The plunging seas draw backward from the land
   Their moon-led waters white.

Alfred Tennyson

MARSHES BY THE SEA

Next appear'd a *dam* – so call the place –
Where lies a road confined in narrow space;
A work of labour, for on either side
Is level fen, a prospect wild and wide,
With dikes on either hand by ocean's self supplied.
Far on the right the distant sea is seen,
And salt the springs that feed the marsh between;
Beneath an ancient bridge, the straiten'd flood
Rolls through its sloping banks of slimy mud;
Near it a sunken boat resists the tide,
That frets and hurries to th' opposing side;
The rushes sharp, that on the borders grow,
Bend their brown flow'rets to the stream below,
Impure in all its course, in all its progress slow:
Here a grave Flora scarcely deigns to bloom,
Nor wears a rosy blush, nor sheds perfume;
The few dull flowers that o'er the place are spread
Partake the nature of their fenny bed;
Here on its wiry stem, in rigid bloom,
Grows the salt lavender that lacks perfume;

Here the dwarf sallows creep, the septfoil harsh,
And the soft slimy mallow of the marsh;
Low on the ear the distant billows sound,
And just in view appears their stony bound;
No hedge nor tree conceals the glowing sun,
Birds, save a wat'ry tribe, the district shun,
Nor chirp among the reeds where bitter waters run.

George Crabbe

Crabbe's sea was the North Sea, like Tennyson's, but further south, off East Anglia; again with marshes behind. Tennyson was one of many poets who have read and read Crabbe for his strong sadness and his landscapes. Edward Thomas said that if Crabbe's low coast of marsh and heath hadn't created Crabbe, it might have been created by Crabbe.

WALKING BY THE SEA

They feel the calm delight, and thus proceed
Through the green lane – then linger in the mead –
Stray o'er the heath in all its purple bloom –
And pluck the blossom where the wild bees hum;
Then through the broomy bound with ease they pass
And press the sandy sheep-walk's slender grass,
Where dwarfish flowers among the gorse are spread,
And the lamb browses by the linnet's bed;
Then 'cross the bounding brook they make their way
O'er its rough bridge – and there behold the bay! –
The ocean smiling to the fervid sun –
The waves that faintly fall and slowly run –
The ships at distance and the boats at hand;
And now they walk upon the sea-side sand,
Counting the number and what kind they be,
Ships softly sinking in the sleepy sea;
Now arm in arm, now parted, they behold
The glitt'ring waters on the shingles roll'd;
The timid girls, half dreading their design,
Dip the small foot in the retarded brine,
And search for crimson weeds, which spreading flow,
Or lie like pictures on the sand below;

With all those bright red pebbles that the sun
Through the small waves so softly shines upon;
And those live lucid jellies which the eye
Delights to trace as they swim glitt'ring by:
Pearl-shells and rubied star-fish they admire,
And will arrange above the parlour-fire.

George Crabbe

JELLYFISH, OR SEA-NETTLES

Now it is pleasant in the summer eve,
When a broad shore retiring waters leave,
Awhile to wait upon the firm fair sand,
When all is calm at sea, all still at land;
And there the ocean's produce to explore,
As floating by, or rolling on the shore;
Those living jellies which the flesh inflame,
Fierce as a nettle, and from that its name;
Some in huge masses, some that you may bring
In the small compass of a lady's ring;
Figured by hand divine – there's not a gem
Wrought by man's art to be compar'd to them;
Soft, brilliant, tender, through the wave they glow,
And make the moonbeam brighter where they flow.

George Crabbe

A JELLYFISH

Visible, invisible,
    a fluctuating charm
an amber-tinctured amethyst
    inhabits it, your arm
approaches and it opens
    and it closes; you had meant
to catch it and it quivers;
    you abandon your intent.

Marianne Moore

THE BEACHÈD VERGE: THE SEA OF
SHAKESPEARE

Say to Athens,
Timon hath made his everlasting mansion
Upon the beachèd verge of the salt flood;
Who once a day with his embossed froth
The turbulent surge shall cover; thither come
And let my grave-stone be your oracle.

William Shakespeare

A beach meant 'shingle', and still does in Kent: a 'beachèd verge' meant a verge made of shingle. Tennyson thinks of sands – Lincolnshire sands smoothing into the sea. Whitman thinks of the low shore and ocean beaches, ocean sands, of Long Island. Shakespeare thinks of the sea frothing on to shingle, on to the 'pibbled' shores of – where? I suppose Kent, remembering *King Lear*, and Edgar, pretending to look down from a cliff near Dover so high that he and Gloucester cannot hear the murmuring surge 'That on th' unnumber'd idle pible chafes.' That's the kind of beach where Timon wants his grave and his monument.

Lie where the light foam of the sea may beat
Thy grave-stone daily, make thine epitaph.

And that's the kind of beach in the sonnet which begins 'Like as the waves make towards the pibled shore', and in *Coriolanus*, – 'the pibbles on the hungry beach.' Perhaps coming down from London to Kent and going over to France from such a rattling beach was Shakespeare's introduction to the sea?

You hear Kentish shingle, Dover shingle, again in the lines by Matthew Arnold, which I shall put last in this sea portion of the book, on page 214.

SEA OF THE BRINE OF LIFE

I behold from the beach your crooked inviting fingers,
I believe you refuse to go back without feeling of me;
We must have a turn together . . . I undress . . . hurry me out of sight
    of the land,
Cushion me soft . . . rock me in billowy drowse,
Dash me with amorous wet . . . I can repay you.

Sea of stretched ground-swells!
Sea breathing broad and convulsive breaths!
Sea of the brine of life! Sea of unshovelled and always-ready graves!
Howler and scooper of storms! Capricious and dainty sea!

Walt Whitman

AFTER THE SEA-SHIP

After the sea-ship, after the whistling winds,
After the white-gray sails taut to their spars and ropes,
Below, a myriad myriad waves hastening, lifting up their necks,
Tending in ceaseless flow toward the track of the ship,
Waves of the ocean bubbling and gurgling, blithely prying,
Waves, undulating waves, liquid, uneven, emulous waves,
Toward that whirling current, laughing and buoyant, with curves,
Where the great vessel sailing and tacking displaced the surface,
Larger and smaller waves in the spread of the ocean yearnfully flowing,
The wake of the sea-ship after she passes, flashing and frolicsome under
    the sun,
A motley procession with many a fleck of foam and many fragments,
Following the stately and rapid ship, in the wake following.

Walt Whitman

LET ME FEEL THEE AGAIN, OLD SEA

Let me feel thee again, old sea! let me leap into thy saddle once more.
I am sick of these terra firma toils and cares; sick of the dust and reek
of towns. Let me hear the clatter of hailstones on icebergs, and not the
dull tramp of these plodders, plodding their dull way from their
cradles to their graves. Let me snuff thee up, sea-breeze! and whinny in
thy spray. Forbid it, sea-gods! intercede for me with Neptune, O sweet
Amphitrite, that no dull clod may fall on my coffin! Be mine the tomb
that swallowed up Pharaoh and all his hosts; let me lie down with
Drake, where he sleeps in the sea.

Herman Melville

THE FISHER'S LOT

Pity, ye Gods, and thaw the rigid frost,
My hands are stiff, and all my feeling lost.
The moon with sharpen'd horns looks coldly bright,
And thus augments the chillness of the night.
Bright icy spangles gild the shining oar,
And snowy flakes have whit'ned all the shore.
How curst the fate! How hard the fisher's lot,
To toil for ever thus, and toil for nought.

William Diaper

THE FISH, THE CHALK CLIFFS AND THE SNOW

When they in throngs a safe retirement seek,
Where pointed rocks the rising surges break,
Or where calm waters in their bason sleep,
While chalky cliffs o'erlook the shaded deep,
The seas all gilded o'er the shoal betray,
And shining tracks inform their wand'ring way.
  As when soft snows, brought down by western gales,
Silent descend and spread on all the vales:
Add to the plains, and on the mountains shine,
While in chang'd fields, the starving cattle pine;
Nature bears all one face, looks coldly bright,
And mourns her lost variety in white,
Unlike themselves the objects glare around,
And with false rays the dazzled sight confound:
So, when the shoal appears, the changing streams
Lose their sky-blue, and shine with silver gleams.

William Diaper

THE PORPOISE

Fair nimble keen-edged porpoise
Leaping lovely waves at will,
Seacalf, brow strangely shaded,
Smooth the way, strange-sounding lad.
Glad you are to be noticed,

Gay on wavecrests near the shore,
A fierce-looking cold-framed head,
Bear's face in frigid currents.
He skips, he shakes like ague,
And then he waggles away,
Black mushroom, wrestles the sea,
Staring at it and snorting.
You are ploughing the breaking
Crests of the waves of the sea;
You split the salty ocean,
Are in the heart of the wave,
Daring shadow, swift and clean.
Skull of the sea, strand's pillion.
He hoes waves, water viper,
His looks give the heart a fright.
You're white-bellied, quite gentle,
Rover of the captive flood.
Boar of the brine, deed of daring,
He roms the sea, long bright trail.
Summers, when weather changes,
You come rocking before storms.
Fierce boar, wild infernal churn,
On wild tides cross and greedy.
Lance with gold-crested breastplate,
Fish in a closely-clasped coat,
Sea's burden, tress on bosom,
He slides, holds on a wave's slope.

From the Welsh of Tomos Prys

After all that the porpoise is asked to swim from the Menai Straits off to Spain, to a Welsh ship's captain, begging him to abandon the sea and come home to his family. Tomos Prys is writing in the old tradition, which he has adapted a little, of asking a bird or a fish or some other creature to take messages of love to a girl. The poets of Wales have liked, not only love messengers, but what is called *dyfalu*, describing something by adding comparison to comparison, likeness to likeness, in a splendid rush of words. This is *dyfalu*, until you have a porpoise complete; and Tomos Prys knew about porpoises, he had certainly watched them racing and playing games. He was an Elizabethan sailor, soldier, adventurer, – and poet. 'He built himself a house on Bardsey Island' – this is the Island of the Saints at the end of the Lleyn peninsula – 'out of the ruins of a monastery, a wild westward facing place where the wind carried sea spray to his mouth every day'.*

HYMN TO THE SEAL

Creature of God, thy coat
That lies all black and fine
I do admire, as on a sunny
Rock to see thee climb.

When thou wast young thy coat
Was pale with spots upon it,
But now in single black it lies
And thou, Seal, liest on it.

What bliss abounds to view
God's creatures in their prime
Climb in full coat upon a rock
To breathe and to recline.

Stevie Smith

SEALS AND SWANS

At this sweet hour, all things beside
  In amorous pairs to covert creep;
The swans that brush the evening tide
  Homeward in snowy couples keep.

In his green den the murmuring seal
  Close by his sleek companion lies;
While singly we to bedward steal,
  And close in fruitless sleep our eyes.

George Darley

These seals and swans, happy in couples, are taken from a song which lonely and disconsolate mermaids sing in the evening. And George Darley was a lonely, disconsolate Irish poet with a stutter.

---

*Gwyn Williams, *An Introduction to Welsh Poetry*.

SEALCHIE SONG

I heard a Mither baing her bairn
An ay she rockit an she sang,
She took sae hard upo' the verse
Till the heart within her body rang.

'O row cradle an go cradle
An ay sleep thon my bairn within.
O little ken I my bairn's faither
Ot yet the land that he liggs in'.

O up then spake a grimly Ghost
A aye sae laigh at her bed's foet.
'O here am I thy bairns faither
Although I'm nae thy luve sae sweet.

Jo Immrannoe it is my name,
Jo Immrannoe they do ca' me,
An' my lands they lie baith braid an' wide
Amang the rocks o' Sule Skerry.

An foster weel my young young son
An' for a twalmont an a day,
An' when the twelmonts fairly done
I'll come an' pay the nourice's fee.'

'But how shall I my young son ken
An' how shall I my young son know?'
"Mang a' the Selkies i' Sule Skerry
He will be midmost among them a'.'

'My husband is a proud gunner
An aye a proud gunner is he,
An' the first shot that he will fire
Will be at my young son an' thee.'

'I fear nae livin' proud gunner,
I fear nae mortal man', quo he,
'For pouther winna burn i' saut
Sae I an' thy young Son'll gae free.'

O when that weary twalmont gaed
He cam to pay the nourice fee,
He had ae coffer fu' o' gowd
An' anither fu' o' white money.

'Upo' the Skerry is thy young son
Upo' the Skerry lieth he.
Sin thou wilt see thy ain young son
Now is the time to speak wi' he.'

The Gunner lay ahind a rock,
Ahind a tangie rock lay he;
An' the very first shot the gunner loot
It strack his wife aboon the bree.

Jo Immrannoe an his young son
Wi heavy hearts took tae the sea.
Let a' that live on mortal lan
Ne'er mell wi' Selchies o' the sea.

Anon

Why shouldn't a seal turn into a man, or the other way round, – if
such things were only possible? The poet Louis MacNeice said to me
once that he would like to change every so often into a seal, and swim
about in a heavy sea, off the rocks. In the Norse islands of the Atlantic
it was believed that the whole race of seals had been men originally.
They came from mortals who had taken their own lives by drowning.
'Once in the year, on Fastern's Eve' – which is Shrove Tuesday, the
last day before the fasting of Lent, Pancake Day – 'they can take off
their skins, and enjoy themselves as human beings, with dancing and
other amusements, in caves and on the flat rocks beside the beach.'*
Various stories say that a man has children by a seal-woman, or – as
in this ballad – that a girl has children by a man who is really a seal.
In the end, the seal-mother or the seal-father goes back for ever into
the sea, and a gunner shoots either seal-parent or seal-child.

This seal-father has his home out in the Atlantic, to the north-west
of Scotland, on the reef called Sule Skerry, the seal skerry; and the
ballad (there is another one like it from Shetland) is in the English of
North Ronaldshay, in Orkney. A sealchie or selkie, of course, is a seal;

---

*W. A. Craigie, *Scandinavian Folk-Lore*.

'liggs' means lies; 'a aye sae laigh' means ever so low; 'nourice' means nurse; 'pouther', powder; 'saut', salt; 'sin', since; 'tangie', covered with tang, which is seaweed; 'loot' means let off, 'aboon the bree' means above the brow, and 'mell' means mix or couple. Yes, and in line one 'baing' means singing ba to the child, singing a lullaby.

In the Scottish islands they say the three fastest things in the sea and the three heroes of the sea are the mackerel, the salmon and the seal.

THE SEA-MAID'S MUSIC

Since once I sat upon a promontory,
And heard a mermaid, on a dolphin's back,
Uttering such dulcet and harmonious breath,
That the rude sea grew civil at her song,
And certain stars shot madly from their spheres,
To hear the sea-maid's music.

William Shakespeare

THE CRUEL, SWEETLY SINGING MERMAIDS

And now they nigh approached to the stead,
  Where as those Mermaids dwelt: it was a still
And calmy bay, on th' one side sheltered
  With the broad shadow of an hoary hill,
  On th' other side an high rock tow'red still,
That twixt them both a pleasaunt port they made,
  And did like an half theatre fulfil:
There those five sisters had continual trade,
And us'd to bath themselves in that deceitful shade.

They were fair ladies, till they fondly striv'd
  With th' Heliconian maids for maistery;
Of whom they over-comen, were depriv'd
  Of their proud beauty, and th' one moiety
  Transform'd to fish, for their bold surquedry,
But th' upper half their hue retained still,
  And their sweet skill in wonted melody;
  Which ever after they abus'd to ill,
T'allure weak travellers, whom gotten they did kill.

So now to Guyon, as he passed by,
    Their pleasaunt tunes they sweetly thus applied;
    O thou fair son of gentle Faery,
    That art in mighty arms most magnified,
    Above all knights, that ever battle tried,
    O turn thy rudder hither-ward a while:
    Here may thy storm-beat vessel safely ride;
    This is the port of rest from troublous toil,
The world's sweet inn, from pain and wearisome turmoil.

With that the rolling sea resounding soft,
    In his big bass them fitly answered,
    And on the rock the waves breaking aloft,
    A calm mean unto them measured,
    The whiles sweet Zephyrus loud whisteled
    His treble, a straunge kind of harmony;
    Which Guyon's senses softly tickeled,
    That he the boatman bade row easily,
And let him hear some part of their rare melody.

                  Edmund Spenser

'Surquedry' is arrogance. 'Mean' is alto or tenor.

Our mermaids – and Spenser's mermaids – come from the Sirens
of the Aegean and the Mediterranean (who sang so sweetly and
dangerously to Ulysses). This does not leave much room in English
poems for mermen and children of mermen and mermaids. But they
exist, in stories from Iceland and Norway and the Faroes. Mermen –
you might expect this from the way their women behave, singing, and
combing their fair hair, and enticing young sailors – are rather ugly
and sulky, dark skinned, smaller than human beings, with long black
beards and very long fingers. They are fish below, of course, like
mermaids. 'The merman . . . lives at the bottom of the sea, and annoys
fishers by biting the bait off the hooks and fixing these in the bottom
so that they have to cut the line. If he is caught, he is so dexterous that
he can loose the thread that ties the hooks to the line, and so escape
from being brought up, and taken on board like any other fish.' That
was what they said in the Faroes. In Norway about these sea people it
was said 'The fishers sometimes catch their children, whom they call
Marmaeler, and take them home with them to get knowledge of the
future from them, for they, as well as the old ones, can foretell things
to come.'* [footnote facing]

BY THE CLEAR GREEN SEA

Sand-strewn caverns, cool and deep,
Where the winds are all asleep;
Where the spent lights quiver and gleam;
Where the salt weed sways in the stream;
Where the sea-beasts rang'd all round
Feed in the ooze of their pasture-ground;
Where the sea-snakes coil and twine,
Dry their mail and bask in the brine;
Where the great whales come sailing by,
Sail and sail, with unshut eye.

Matthew Arnold

JONAH IN THE WHALE

A cream of phosphorescent light
Floats on the wash that to and fro
Slides round his feet – enough to show
Many a pendulous stalactite
Of naked mucous, whorls and wreaths
And huge festoons of mottled tripes
And smaller palpitating pipes
Through which a yeasty liquor seethes.

Seated upon the convex mound
Of one vast kidney, Jonah prays
And sings his canticles and hymns
Making the hollow vault resound
God's goodness and mysterious ways,
Till the great fish spouts music as he swims.

Aldous Huxley

From that poem I remember always the mottled tripes and Jonah
sitting enjoying himself on the whale's kidney. Jonah wasn't so happy
in every poem. Could Aldous Huxley have read the lines he was made
to exclaim in a very odd *Historie of Jonah*, by a minister of Glasgow
University, Zachary Boyd, in Cromwell's time? Jonah is in the whale:

---

*Both quotations I have taken from W. A. Craigie's *Scandinavian Folk Lore*.

What house is this, where's neither fire nor candle,
Where I no thing but guts of fishes handle?
I, and my table, are both heere within,
Where day ne'er dawn'd, where sun did never shine.
The like of this on earth man never saw,
A living man within a monster's mawe;
Buried under mountaines which are high and steep,
Plung'd under water hundrethe fathomes deep . . .
In all the earth like unto mee is none,
Farre from all living I heere lye alone,
Where I entomb'd in melancholy sink,
Choak't, suffocat, with excremental stink.
This grieves mee most, that I for grievous sinne,
Incarc'rd lye within this floating Inn.

DEGREES OF STRENGTH

Strong is the horse upon his speed;
Strong in pursuit the rapid glede,
    Which makes at once his game:
Strong the tall ostrich on the ground;
Strong through the turbulent profound
    Shoots xiphias to his aim.

Strong is the lion – like a coal
His eyeball – like a bastion's mole
    His chest against the foes:
Strong the gier-eagle on his sail,
Strong against tide, th' enormous whale
    Emerges as he goes.

But stronger still, in earth and air,
And in the sea, the man of pray'r,
    And far beneath the tide;
And in the seat to faith assign'd,
Where ask is have, where seek is find,
    Where knock is open wide.

Christopher Smart

Glede: the kite, which used to be common in England. xiphias: the
swordfish. The man of prayer beneath the tide is Jonah in the whale.

THE SEA ON FIRE

*(Having abandoned their brigantine three men are sailing
in an open boat through the Pacific)*

The night following our abandonment of the Parki was made memorable by a remarkable spectacle.

Slumbering in the bottom of the boat, Jarl and I were suddenly awakened by Samoa. Starting, we beheld the ocean of a pallid white colour, corruscating all over with tiny golden sparkles. But the pervading hue of the water cast a cadaverous gleam upon the boat, so that we looked to each other like ghosts. For many rods astern our wake was revealed in a line of rushing illuminated foam; while here and there beneath the surface, the tracks of sharks were denoted by vivid, greenish trails, crossing and recrossing each other in every direction. Farther away, and distributed in clusters, floated on the sea like constellations in the heavens, innumerable Medusae, a species of small, round, refulgent fish, only to be met with in the South Seas and the Indian Ocean.

Suddenly as we gazed there shot high into the air a bushy jet of flashes, accompanied by the unmistakable deep breathing sound of a sperm whale. Soon the sea all round us spouted in fountains of fire; and vast forms, emitting a glare from their flanks, and ever and anon raising their heads above water and shaking off the sparkles, showed where an immense shoal of Cachalots had risen from below to sport in these phosphorescent billows.

The vapours jetted forth was far more radiant than any portion of the sea; ascribable perhaps to the originally luminous fluid contracting still more brilliancy from its passage through the spouting canal of the whales.

We were in great fear, lest without any vicious intention the leviathans might destroy us by coming into close contact with our boat. We would have shunned them; but they were all round and round us. Nevertheless we were safe; for as we parted the pallid brine, the peculiar irradiation which shot from about our keel seemed to deter them. Apparently discovering us of a sudden, many of them plunged headlong down into the water, tossing their fiery tails high into the air and leaving the sea still more sparkling from the violent surging of their descent.

Herman Melville

WHALES

The dawn of day;
Whales bellow
In the icy sea.

After the Japanese of Gyōdai

Do whales bellow? I thought you might ask, doubtfully; and of course
they don't. But whales are not altogether silent. Some of the small
whales have been heard to scream, howl, grunt, moan. The huge Sperm
Whale has been heard to whistle and squeak and make clicking noises.
But bellowing is another thing. Perhaps Gyōdai – who lived in a
country of islands where they know about whales and whaling – meant
rumblings or breathings through the nose, through the blowhole. Let's
say he imagined whales bellowing – it makes his sea all the more icy,
and his dawn all the stranger.

Herman Melville maintained that the whale has no voice – 'unless
you insult him by saying that when he so strangely rumbles, he talks
through his nose. But then again, what has the whale to say? Seldom
have I known any profound being that had anything to say to this
world, unless forced to stammer out something by way of getting a
living.'

THE WHALERS

I sought the men return'd from regions cold,
The frozen straits, where icy mountains roll'd;
Some I could win to tell me serious tales
Of boats uplifted by enormous whales,
Or, when harpoon'd, how swiftly through the sea
The wounded monsters with the cordage flee.
Yet some uneasy thoughts assail'd me then:
The smaller fry we take, with scales and fins,
Who gasp and die – this adds not to our sins;
But so much blood, warm life, and frames so large
To strike, to murder – seem'd an heavy charge.
    They told of days, where many goes to one –
Such days as ours; and how a larger sun,
Red, but not flaming, roll'd, with motion slow,
On the world's edge, and never dropt below.

George Crabbe

(It isn't Crabbe, I should say in fairness to him, but the protagonist of one of his tales who is distinguishing between large deaths and small deaths.)

THE DAY IS DARK AND BLACK THE SEA

The snow lies sprinkled on the beach,
And whitens all the marshy lea:
The sad gulls wail adown the gale,
The day is dark and black the sea.
    Shorn of their crests the blighted waves
With driven foam the offing fleck:
The ebb is low and barely laves
The red rust of the giant wreck.

Robert Bridges

THE DEEP MOANS ROUND

The lights begin to twinkle from the rocks:
The long day wanes: the slow moon climbs: the deep
Moans round with many voices.

Alfred Tennyson

Lincolnshire sea, again, in Tennyson's mind, though he is writing about Ulysses? In the next sea-piece, from *Enoch Arden*, the seas coloured like lead sway round the Isle of Wight, below Tennyson's house there on the downs.

After that comes *Break, Break, Break*, which he wrote in Lincolnshire. ('It was made in a Lincolnshire lane,' Tennyson said, 'at five o'clock in the morning.')

NOVEMBER SEAS

November dawns and dewy-glooming downs,
The gentle shower, the smell of dying leaves,
And the low moan of leaden-colour'd seas.

Alfred Tennyson

BREAK, BREAK, BREAK

Break, break, break,
 On thy cold gray stones, O sea!
And I would that my tongue could utter
 The thoughts that arise in me.

O well for the fisherman's boy,
 That he shouts with his sister at play!
O well for the sailor lad,
 That he sings in his boat on the bay!

And the stately ships go on
 To their haven under the hill;
But O for the touch of a vanished hand,
 And the sound of a voice that is still!

Break, break, break,
 At the foot of thy crags, O Sea!
But the tender grace of a day that is dead
 Will never come back to me.

Alfred Tennyson

FROM 'DOVER BEACH'

The sea is calm to-night,
The tide is full, the moon lies fair
Upon the straits; on the French coast the light
Gleams and is gone; the cliffs of England stand,
Glimmering and vast, out in the tranquil bay.
Come to the window, sweet is the night-air!
Only, from the long line of spray
Where the sea meets the moon-blanched land,
Listen! you hear the grating roar
Of pebbles which the waves draw back, and fling,
At their return up the high strand,
Begin, and cease, and then again begin,
With tremulous cadence slow, and bring
The eternal note of sadness in.

Matthew Arnold

9 · *Autumn, then winter, frost, ice and snow*

MORNING GLORIES IN AUTUMN
(from Japan)

i
The autumn of wind;
It shows the back
Of the Morning Glories.
Kyoroku

ii
On the dust heap
Morning Glories are flowering
At the close of autumn.
Taigi

Till frosts begin, Morning Glories are particularly splendid in a clear autumn, when there are no longer many other flowers. The pain is that such blue, blue objects, intimately open at eye level, won't come out for much longer; which explains (if you look back to page 75) why Morning Glory is a season word in these short Japanese poems. And before the weather breaks you notice the wind turning the flowers, or you notice – with surprise – that there are Morning Glory flowers wide open on the rubbish heap where the vines were thrown away the autumn before, or in a tangle of weeds or grass where the Morning Glories happened to seed themselves last year.

A SONG TO THE DECAYING YEAR

Now I am minded to take pipe in hand
And yield a song to the decaying year;
Now while the full-leaved hursts unalter'd stand,
    And scarcely does appear
The Autumn yellow feather in the boughs
    While there is neither sun nor rain;
And a grey heaven does the hush'd earth house,
And bluer grey the flocks of trees look in the plain.
So late the hoar green chestnut breaks a bud,
And feeds new leaves upon the winds of Fall;
So late there is no force in sap or blood;
    The fruit against the wall
Loose on the stem has done its summering;

These should have starv'd with the green broods of spring,
    Or never been at all;
Too late or else much, much too soon,
Who first knew moonlight by the hunters' moon.

Gerard Manley Hopkins

IN A SILENT AUTUMN NIGHT

Lo! sweetened with the summer light,
The full-juiced apple waxing over-mellow,
Drops in a silent autumn night.

Alfred Tennyson

FAIR IS THE WORLD

Fair is the world, now autumn's wearing,
And the sluggard sun lies long abed;
Sweet are the days, now winter's nearing,
And all winds feign that the wind is dead.

Dumb is the hedge where the crabs hang yellow,
Bright as the blossoms of the spring;
Dumb is the close where the pears hang mellow,
And none but the dauntless redbreasts sing.

Fair was the spring, but amidst his greening
Grey were the days of the hidden sun;
Fair was the summer, but overweening,
So soon his o'er-sweet days were done.

Come then, love, for peace is upon us,
Far off is failing, and far is fear,
Here where the rest in the end hath won us,
In the gathering tide of the happy year.

Come from the grey old house by the water,
Where, far from the lips of the hungry sea,
Green groweth the grass o'er the field of the slaughter,
And all is a tale for thee and me.

William Morris

I REMEMBER A CLEAR MORNING

I remember a clear morning in the Ninth Month when it had been raining all night. Despite the bright sun, dew was still dripping from the chrysanthemums in the garden. On the bamboo fences and criss-cross hedges I saw tatters of spider webs; and where the threads were broken the raindrops hung on them like strings of white pearls. I was greatly moved and delighted.

As it became sunnier, the dew gradually vanished from the clover and the other plants where it had lain so heavily; the branches began to stir, then suddenly sprang up of their own accord. Later I described to people how beautiful it all was. What most impressed me was that they were not at all impressed.

Sei Shōnagon

THAT TIME OF YEAR THOU MAYST
IN ME BEHOLD

That time of year thou mayst in me behold
  When yellow leaves, or none, or few, do hang
Upon those boughs which shake against the cold,
  Bare ruined choirs, where late the sweet birds sang.
In me thou see'st the twilight of such day
  As after sunset fadeth in the west;
Which by and by black night doth take away,
  Death's second self, that seals up all the rest.
In me thou see'st the glowing of such fire,
  That on the ashes of his youth doth lie,
As the death-bed whereon it must expire,
  Consumed with that which it was nourished by.
    This thou perceivest, which makes thy love more strong,
    To love that well which thou must leave ere long.

William Shakespeare

AN AUTUMN MORNING

The autumn morning, waked by many a gun,
Throws o'er the fields her many-coloured light.
Wood wildly touched, close tanned, and stubbles dun,
A motley paradise for earth's delight;
Clouds ripple as the darkness breaks to light,

And clover plots are hid with silver mist,
One shower of cobwebs o'er the surface spread;
And threads of silk in strange disorder twist
Round every leaf and blossom's bottly head;
Hares in the drowning herbage scarcely steal
But on the battered pathway squat abed
And by the cart-rut nip their morning meal.
Look where we may, the scene is strange and new,
And every object wears a changing hue.

John Clare

CALM IS THE MORN WITHOUT A SOUND

Calm is the morn without a sound,
   Calm as to suit a calmer grief,
   And only thro' the faded leaf
The chestnut pattering to the ground;

Calm and deep peace on this high wold,
   And on these dews that drench the furze,
   And all the silvery gossamers
That twinkle into green and gold;

Calm and still light on yon great plain
   That sweeps with all its autumn bowers,
   And crowded farms and lessening towers,
To mingle with the bounding main;

Calm and deep peace in this wide air,
   These leaves that redden to the fall,
   And in my heart, if calm at all,
If any calm, a calm despair;

Calm on the seas, and silver sleep,
   And waves that sway themselves in rest,
   And dead calm in the noble breast
Which heaves but with the heaving deep.

Alfred Tennyson

The last two lines may be puzzling even if you know that this is one
poem out of the long sequence, *In Memoriam*, in which Tennyson is

remembering his dead friend Arthur Hallam. He had died on the land, at Vienna, but his body was being brought back to England by sea, from Trieste. So the noble breast heaves but with the heaving deep.

SADNESS OF AUTUMN

Early he rose, and look'd with many a sigh
On the red light that fill'd the eastern sky;
Oft had he stood before, alert and gay,
To hail the glories of the new-born day;
But now dejected, languid, listless, low,
He saw the wind upon the water blow,
And the cold stream curl'd onward as the gale
From the pine-hill blew harshly down the dale.
On the right side the youth a wood survey'd,
With all its dark intensity of shade;
Where the rough wind alone was heard to move,
In this, the pause of nature and of love,
When now the young are rear'd, and when the old,
Lost to the tie, grow negligent and cold –
Far to the left he saw the huts of men,
Half hid in mist, that hung upon the fen;
Before him swallows, gathering for the sea,
Took their short flights, and twitter'd on the lea;
And near the bean-sheaf stood, the harvest done,
And slowly blacken'd in the sickly sun;
All these were sad in nature, or they took
Sadness from him, the likeness of his look,

George Crabbe

The story I like best about admiring Crabbe should come here, after the landscape by him that was Tennyson's favourite. Tennyson read I think the tale which this comes from, to some of his friends, finished it, looked round, and said in reproach 'I do not see any of you weeping'.

Then Wordsworth – Wordsworth went for walks with Crabbe on Hampstead Heath, looking down on to London capped with smoke: he wrote*

---

*In *Extempora Effusion upon the Death of James Hogg*.

Our haughty life is crowned with darkness,
Like London with its own black wreath,
On which with thee, O Crabbe! forth-looking,
I gazed from Hampstead's breezy heath.

(The landscape in the sickly sun takes on its extra sadness in the poem because, as Crabbe explains, the young man who looks across the fen, has just foolishly and inextricably engaged himself to a girl he doesn't want to marry.)

HARVEST MOON

Harvest moon!
The smoke steals
Over the water.

After the Japanese of Ransetsu

Smoke visible at night, smoke visible in the full light of the harvest moon, over moonlit water, moving slowly when there is next to no wind.

THEN SHALL TH' AUTUMNAL YELLOW CLOTHE THE LEAF

Unnumber'd violets on those banks appear,
And all the first-born beauties of the year;
The grey-green blossoms of the willow bring
The large wild bees upon the labouring wing.
Then comes the summer with augmented pride,
Whose pure small streams along the valley glide;
Her richer Flora their brief charms display,
And, as the fruit advances, fall away.
Then shall th' autumnal yellow clothe the leaf,
What time the reaper binds the burden'd sheaf;
Then silent groves denote the dying year,
The morning frost, the noon-tide gossamer;
And all be silent in the scene around –
All, save the distant sea's uncertain sound,
Or here and there the gun, whose loud report
Proclaims to man that Death is but his sport.

And then the wintry winds begin to blow;
Then fall the flaky stars of gathering snow;
When on the thorn the ripening sloe, yet blue,
Takes the bright varnish of the morning dew;
The aged moss grows brittle on the pale;
And dry boughs splinter in the wintry gale;
And every changing season of the year
Stamps on the scene its English character.

George Crabbe

MORNING MUSHROOMS

Now mushrooms with the morning light
Above the wet grass glisten white.

John Clare

MUSHROOMS OF AUTUMN

Lovelier far than vernal flow'rs
Thy mushrooms shooting after show'rs;
That fear no more the fatal scythe,
But proudly spread their bonnets blythe,
With coverings form'd of silk and snow,
And lin'd with brightening pink below . . .
But more the later fungus race,
Begot by Phoebus' warm embrace,
In summer months, on procreant earth,
By damp September brought to birth; . . .
Their forms and hues some solace yield,
In wood, or wild, or humid field;
Whose tapering stems, robust, or light,
Like columns catch the searching sight,
To claim remark where e'er I roam;
Supporting each a shapely dome;
Like fair umbrellas, furl'd, or spread,
Display their many-colour'd head;
Grey, purple, yellow, white, or brown,
Shap'd like war's shield, or prelate's crown –
Like freedom's cap, or friar's cowl,
Or china's bright inverted bowl –

And while their broadening disks unfold
Gay silvery gills, or nets of gold,
Beneath their shady, curtain'd cove,
Perform all offices of love.

James Woodhouse

No one much remembers James Woodhouse. He began by making
and mending shoes, he made poems, Dr Johnson sneered at them,
Wordsworth liked a few of them, including, I think, these mushroomy
lines, from which you wouldn't guess that he was a huge man, six
feet six inches tall, who had 27 children, once knocked down a bull
with a stick, and lived – from 1735 to 1820 – to be eighty-five. Few
poets have noticed fungi, which are beautiful things, and there are
fewer poisonous kinds of mushroom than poisonous kinds of flower.
But then it does not do to be called fungus or toadstool.

The poem which follows is mushrooms, Stonehenge, snails and
time, all four.

THE FAIRY RING

Here the horse-mushrooms make a fairy ring.
   Some standing upright and some overthrown,
A small Stonehenge, where heavy black snails cling
   And bite away, like Time, the tender stone.

Andrew Young

A MUSHROOM

   A mushroom: stuck
To it a leaf
   From a tree somewhere.

After the Japanese of Bashō

AUTUMN MIST

i

So thick a mist hung over all,
Rain had no room to fall;
It seemed a sea without a shore;
The cobwebs drooped heavy and hoar
As though with wool they had been knit;
Too obvious mark for fly to hit!

And though the sun was somewhere else
The gloom had brightness of its own
That shone on bracken, grass and stone
And mole-mound with its broken shells
That told where squirrel lately sat,
Cracked hazel-nuts and ate the fat.

And sullen haws in the hedgerows
Burned in the damp with clearer fire;
And brighter still than those
The scarlet hips hung on the briar
Like coffins of the dead dog-rose;
All were as bright as though for earth
Death were a gayer thing than birth.

Andrew Young

ii

The hanging raindrops
Have not dried from the needles
Of the fir forest
Before the evening mist
Of Autumn rises.

From the Japanese of the monk Jakuren

THE DEAD LEAF

On the nigh-naked tree the robin piped
Disconsolate, and through the dripping haze
The dead weight of the dead leaf bore it down:
Thicker the drizzle grew, deeper the gloom.

Alfred Tennyson

ICE

The North Wind sighed:
And in a trice
What was water
Now is ice.

What sweet rippling
Water was
Now bewitched is
Into glass:

White and brittle
Where is seen
The prisoned milfoil's
Tender green;

Clear and ringing,
With sun aglow,
Where the boys sliding
And skating go.

Now furred's each stick
And stalk and blade
With crystals out of
Dewdrops made.

Worms and ants,
Flies, snails and bees
Keep close house-guard,
Lest they freeze;

Oh, with how sad
And solemn an eye
Each fish stares up
Into the sky,

In dread lest his
Wide watery home
At night shall solid
Ice become.

Walter de la Mare

FROST AND SNOW

For never resting time leads summer on
To hideous winter and confounds him there;
Sap checkt with frost, and lusty leaves quite gone,
Beauty o'ersnow'd, and bareness every where.

William Shakespeare

THE RED FOOTBALL

The woodman gladly views the closing day,
To see the sun drop down behind the wood,
Sinking in clouds deep blue or misty grey,
Round as a foot-ball and as red as blood:
The pleasing prospect does his heart much good,
Though 'tis not his such beauties to admire;
He hastes to fill his bags with billet-wood,
Well-pleas'd from the chill prospect to retire,
To seek his corner chair, and warm snug cottage fire.

John Clare

This winter sun may be telling the woodman that his day's work is over, but the great visible thing is the sun as it goes down. Clare was a sun poet. He was bred in flat country, he knew the moments when the sun itself can be looked at for a moment, a globe rising or setting. In his great poem 'A Vision', which he wrote in an interval in madness, he spoke of snatching the eternal ray of the sun and using it as a pen with which he writes his name into immortality and freedom.

A poem he wrote when he was young begins 'Welcome, red and roundy sun', a line one remembers. And see his sun poem on page 36.

THE RUFFIAN WINTER FREEZES THE RIVER DOVE, IN THE GREAT FROST OF 1683

How have I this while forgot so
My mistress Dove, who went to pot too,
My white Dove that was smoking ever
In spite of Winter's worst endeavour,
And still could so evade or fly him
As never to be pinion'd by him,

Now numb'd with bitterness of weather,
Had not the pow'r to stir a feather,
Wherein the nymph was to be pitied,
But flagg'd her wings and so submitted.
The ruffian bound, though, knowing's betters,
Her silver feet in crystal fetters,
In which estate we saw poor Dove lie
Even in captivity more lovely:
But in the fate of this bright princess
Reason itself you know convinces
That her pinniferous fry must die all,
Imprison'd in the crystal vial;
And doubtless there was great mortality
Of trout and grayling of great quality,
Whom love and honour did importune
To stick to her in her misfortune,
Though we shall find, no doubt, good dishes
Next summer of plebeian fishes.

Charles Cotton

WHILE THE DUMB RIVERS SLOWLY FLOAT

Sees not my friend, what a deep snow
Candies our country's woody brow?
The yielding branch his load scarce bears
Opprest with snow, and frozen tears,
While the dumb rivers slowly float,
All bound up in an icy coat.

Henry Vaughan

THE SUNBEAM SAID, BE HAPPY

Bleak season was it, turbulent and bleak,
When hitherward we journeyed, side by side,
Through bursts of sunshine and through flying showers,
Paced the long Vales, how long they were, and yet
How fast that length of way was left behind,
    Wensley's rich Vale and Sedbergh's naked heights.
The frosty wind, as if to make amends
For its keen breath, was aiding to our steps,

And drove us onward like two ships at sea,
Or like two Birds, companions in mid air,
Parted and re-united by the blast.
Stern was the face of Nature; we rejoiced
In that stern countenance, for our Souls thence drew
A feeling of their strength. The naked Trees,
The icy brooks, as on we passed, appeared
To question us. 'Whence come ye? to what end?'
They seemed to say; 'What would ye,' said the shower,
'Wild Wanderers, whither through my dark domain?'
The sunbeam said, 'be happy'. When this Vale
We entered, bright and solemn was the sky
That faced us with a passionate welcoming,
And led us to our threshold.

William Wordsworth

After a wild December journey of four days, on horseback, on foot, in a cart, and then in a carriage, William Wordsworth and his sister Dorothy reach Grasmere, happiness, and the cottage where they were to live and where Wordsworth was to write many of his poems. It was 1799, Wordsworth was twenty-nine, Dorothy twenty-eight. The cottage had been an inn called The Dove and Olive Branch (see page 88), and it was now known as Dove Cottage. The name must have pleased the two Wordsworths. About his sister Wordsworth wrote that wherever his footsteps turned

Her Voice was like a hidden Bird that sang,
The thought of her was like a flash of light,
Or an *unseen* companionship, a breath,
Or fragrance independent of the wind.

He felt, now he was in Dove Cottage, a brightness inside himself, something unique, 'That must not die, that must not pass away', which he would give to all the world.

WINTER COLD

Cold, cold,
cold to-night is wide Magh Luirg;
The snow is higher than a mountain,
the deer cannot get at its food.

Deathly cold;
the storm has spread on every side;
each sloping furrow is a river
and every ford is a full mere.

Each full lake is a great sea,
and each mere is a full lake;
horses cannot get across the ford of Ross,
no more can two feet get there.

The fishes of Ireland are a-roving,
there is not a strand whereon the wave does not dash,
there is not a town in the land.
no bell is to be heard, no crane calls.

The wolves of Cuan Wood do not get
repose or sleep in the lair of wolves;
the little wren does not find
shelter for her nest on the slope of Lon.

The keen wind and the cold ice
have broken out on the company of little birds;
the blackbird does not find a bank she would like,
shelter for her side in the woods of Cuan.

Snug in our cauldron on its hook,
ramshackle the hut on the slope of Lon;
snow has crushed the wood here,
it is difficult to climb up Benn Bó.

The eagle of brown Glen Ridhe
gets affliction from the bitter wind;
great is her misery and her suffering,
the ice will get into her beak.

It is foolish for you – take heed of it –
to rise from quilt and feather-bed;
there is much ice on every ford;
that is why I say 'Cold'.

Anon (from the Old Irish)

There is a story here, round the poem. Under the quilt, snug in the feather-bed, were Diarmuid and Grania, the lovers of Irish legend, who had run away from the great Finn and his Fenians (you know the poem about them by Yeats, the *Faery Song*, beginning

We who are old, old and grey,
O so old,
Thousands of years, thousands of years
If all were told – ?)

The poem is supposed to be said or sung to Diarmuid and Grania by an old woman in whose house they had taken shelter. She wants to betray them to Finn, so she goes on about the cold outside, the snow, the full fords, the wolves and the wind and the ice.

WINTER'S FROSTY PANGS

Come then! and while the slow icicle hangs
At the stiff thatch, and Winter's frosty pangs
Benumb the year, blithe (as of old) let us
'Midst noise and war, of peace, and mirth discuss.
This portion thou wert born for: why should we
Vex at the time's ridiculous misery?

Henry Vaughan

Vaughan is inviting a friend to make him a winter visit, during the Civil War, – which is 'the time's ridiculous misery'. Being Vaughan he cannot resist giving a picture of the weather out of doors, the icicles hanging from the stiff straw of his roof.

THE SILENT ICICLES

> All seasons shall be sweet to thee,
> Whether the summer clothe the general earth
> With greenness, or the redbreast sit and sing
> Betwixt the tufts of snow on the bare branch
> Of mossy apple-tree, while the nigh thatch
> Smokes in the sun-thaw; whether the eave-drops fall
> Heard only in the trances of the blast,
> Or if the secret ministry of frost
> Shall hang them up in silent icicles
> Quietly shining to the quiet Moon.
>
> S. T. Coleridge

Coleridge, Vaughan, Wordsworth, Milton, Tennyson, Hopkins, de la
Mare – gleam always arrests them, by night (our problem is often to
escape from the vast glows or innumerable twinklings of artificial
light into real night where stars, or glow-worms, or fire-flies, or
illumination by the moon are not interfered with) or by day. To those
shining icicles, I shall add from Coleridge a gleam of ice in daylight,
Coleridge in his notebook, for January 3, 1804: 'Remember to describe
water . . . pulsating/really gliding down under ice/water – black under
ice – silver.' In his frost world he would mention his pleasure, as well,
in the echoing noise from kicking frozen horsedung. We can kick
frozen cowpats, if there are few horses any more.

DIAMOND WOODS REFLECTED IN THE LAKE

> How vast the compass of this theatre,
> Yet nothing to be seen but lovely pomp
> And silent majesty; the birch-tree woods
> Are hung with thousand thousand diamond drops
> Of melted hoar-frost, every tiny knot
> In the bare twigs, each little budding-place
> Cased with its several bead, what myriads there
> Upon one tree, while all the distant grove
> That rises to the summit of the steep
> Shows like a mountain built of silver light.
> See yonder the same pageant, and again
> Behold the universal imagery

Inverted, all its sun-bright features touched
As with the varnish, and the gloss of dreams;
Dreamlike the blending also of the whole
Harmonious landscape; all along the shore
The boundary lost, the line invisible
That parts the image from reality;
And the clear hills, as high as they ascend
Heavenward, so piercing deep the lake below.

William Wordsworth

RIDDLE

When it through the wood doth go,
It touches every twig below.

(*Snow*)

THE SNOW

I do not sleep at night nor go out by day, I am sad because the world
has disappeared, nor is there ford nor bank left, nor open ground nor
fields. Nor will I be enticed out of my house by any girl's invitation
while this plague continues, this cloak of white feathers sticking close
like dragon's scales, but tell her that I do not want my coat made white
like a miller's garment. After New Year one must go wrapped in fur,
and during January God makes us start the year as hermits.

Now God has whitewashed the dark earth all around till there is no
undergrowth without its white garment, no coppins that's not covered
with a sheet: fine flour has been milled on every stump, heavenly flour
like April blossoms. A cold veil lies over the woods and the young
trees, a load of chalk bows down the trees; ghostly wheaten flour
which falls till a white coat of mail covers all the fields of the plain.
The soil of the ploughed fields is covered with a cold grit, lying like a
thick coat of tallow on the earth's skin, and a shower of frozen foam
falls in fleeces big as a man's fist. Across North Wales the snowflakes
wander like a swarm of white bees. Why does God throw down this
mass of feathers like the down of his own geese, till here below the
drifts sway and billow over the heather like swollen bellies big as heaps
of chaff and covered with ermine? The dust piles in a drift where we
sang along the pleasant paths.

Will someone who knows tell me what people spit down on earth in January or are they angels sawing timber in heaven? See how they lift their planks in the flour-loft and shake the dust down on us: and they wear cloaks of frosty silver trimmed with coldest quicksilver.

This garment of snow holds us in its grip while it remains cementing together hills, valleys and ditches under a steel coat fit to break the earth, fixing all into a vast monument greater than the graveyard of the sea. What a great fall lies on my country, a white wall stretching from one sea to another! Who dares fight its rude power? A leaden cloak lies on us. When will the rain come?

Anon (from the medieval Welsh)

A Welsh poem with *dyfalu* once more (page 203), many, many riddlings and comparisons to establish the nature, the whiteness and the surprise and the inconvenience of snow.

SNOW IN THE SUBURBS

Every branch big with it,
Bent every twig with it;
Every fork like a white web-foot;
Every street and pavement mute:
Some flakes have lost their way, and grope back upward, when
Meeting those meandering down they turn and descend again.
The palings are glued together like a wall,
And there is no waft of wind with the fleecy fall.

A sparrow enters the tree,
Whereupon immediately
A snow-lump thrice his own slight size
Descends on him and showers his head and eyes,
And overturns him,
And near inurns him,
And lights on a nether twig, when its brush
Starts off a volley of other lodging lumps with a rush.

The steps are a blanched slope,
Up which, with feeble hope,
A black cat comes, wide-eyed and thin;
And we take him in.

Thomas Hardy

SNOW

Ridged thickly on black bough
　　And foaming on twig-fork in swollen lumps
At flirt of bird-wing or wind's sough
　　Plump snow tumbled on snow softly with sudden dumps.

Where early steps had made
　　A wavering track through the white-blotted road
Breaking its brightness with blue shade,
　　Snow creaked beneath my feet with snow heavily shod.

I reached a snow-thatched rick
　　Where men sawed bedding off for horse and cow;
There varnished straws were lying thick
　　Paving with streaky gold the trodden silver snow.

Such light filled me with awe
　　And nothing marred my paradisal thought,
That robin least of all I saw
　　Lying too fast asleep, his song choked in his throat.

Andrew Young

THE SIGNPOST

Snowflakes dance on the night;
　　A single star
Glows with a wide blue light
　　On Lochnagar.

Through snow-fields trails the Dee;
　　At the wind's breath
An ermine-clad spruce-tree
　　Spits snow beneath.

White-armed at the roadside
　　Wails a signpost,
'To-night the world has died
　　And left its ghost.'

Andrew Young

OAKS IN THE SNOW

How strange the wood appears in dark and white,
  And every little twig is hung with snow;
  The old oak tops, crampt, gnarled, and dark below,
Upon their upper sides are fringed in light.

         John Clare

SNOWING

Day darkens,
And once more it begins
To snow.

   After the Japanese of Gyōdai

Remember Walter de la Mare summing up the cold, all the cold, at
the end of one of his poems* by imagining that the North sighs out his
final line

   '*Snow, snow, more snow!*'

A PATCH OF OLD SNOW

There's a patch of old snow in a corner
  That I should have guessed
Was a blow-away paper the rain
  Had brought to rest.

It is speckled with grime as if
  Small print overspread it,
The news of a day I've forgotten –
  If I ever read it.

         Robert Frost

Coleridge's son Hartley (in whose eye the moonlight had glittered,
page 55), living waywardly and without hold of himself, wrote† that
he was

   Untimely old, irreverently grey,
   Much like a patch of dusty snow in May.

---

*Winter.
†In the sonnet *How shall a man fore-doomed to lone estate.*

It is always surprising and moving to see snow past its time. Perhaps Robert Frost's poem about such snow should have been included in the portion of this book given to the spring and the summer.

ALL THE STARS

All the various stars
Appearing,
Ah, the cold!

After the Japanese of Taigi

10 · *About ourselves, who are also nature*

THERE WAS A CHILD WENT FORTH

There was a child went forth every day,
And the first object he looked upon and received with wonder or pity
  or love or dread, that object he became,
And that object became part of him for the day or a certain part or the
  day ... or for many years or stretching cycles of years.

The early lilacs became part of this child,
And grass, and white and red morning glories, and white and red clover,
  and the song of the phoebe-bird,
And the March-born lambs, and the sow's pink-faint litter, and the
  mare's foal, and the cow's calf, and the noisy brood of the barnyard
  or by the mire of the pondside ... and the fish suspending them-
  selves so curiously below there ... and the beautiful curious liquid
  ... and the water-plants with their graceful flat heads ... all became
  part of him.

And the field-sprouts of April and May became part of him ... winter-
  grain sprouts, and those of the light-yellow corn, and of the esculent
  roots of the garden,
And the appletrees covered with blossoms, and the fruit afterward
  ... and woodberries ... and the commonest weeds by the road;
And the old drunkard staggering home from the outhouse of the
  tavern whence he had lately risen,
And the schoolmistress that passed on her way to the school ... and
  the friendly boys that passed ... and the quarrelsome boys ... and
  the tidy and freshcheeked girls ... and the barefoot negro boy and
  girl,
And all the changes of city and country wherever he went.

Walt Whitman

THE POET

Fresh and rosy red the sun is mounting high,
On floats the sea in distant blue careering through its channels,
On floats the wind over the breast of the sea setting in toward land,
The great steady wind from west or west-by-south,
Floating so buoyant with milk-white foam on the waters.

But I am not the sea nor the red sun,
I am not the wind with girlish laughter,
Not the immense wind which strengthens, not the wind which lashes,
Not the spirit that ever lashes its own body to terror and death,
But I am that which unseen comes and sings, sings, sings,
Which babbles in brooks and scoots in showers on the land,
Which the birds know in the woods mornings and evenings,
And the shore-sands know and the hissing wave, and that banner and
    pennant,
Aloft there flapping and flapping.

Walt Whitman

You can say all poems portray, or betray, the poets who write them,
and so all poems are about the nature of man. But sometimes poets
write about themselves directly and deliberately, as painters often paint
themselves. There you have had Walt Whitman on what made him, he
believed, and what he felt himself to have become, and in the same way
the next few poems will be poet-portraits, chiefly self-portraits.

I AM THE POET DAVIES, WILLIAM

I am the Poet Davies, William,
   I sin without a blush or blink:
I am a man that lives to eat;
   I am a man that lives to drink.

My face is large, my lips are thick,
   My skin is coarse and black almost;
But the ugliest feature is my verse,
   Which proves my soul is black and lost.

Thank heaven thou didst not marry me,
   A poet full of blackest evil;
For how to manage my damned soul
   Will puzzle many a flaming devil.

W. H. Davies

ANOTHER POET FROM WALES

I was told by a very sober and knowing person (now dead) that in his time there was a young lad father and motherless, and so very poor that he was forced to beg; but at last was taken up by a rich man, that kept a great stock of sheep upon the mountains not far from the place where I now dwell, who clothed him and sent him into the mountains to keep his sheep. There in summer time following the sheep and looking to their lambs, he fell into a deep sleep; in which he dreamt, that he saw a beautiful young man with a garland of green leafs upon his head, and an hawk upon his fist; with a quiver full of arrows at his back, coming towards him (whistling several measures or tunes all the way) and at last let the hawk fly at him, which (he dreamt) got into his mouth and inward parts, and suddenly awaked in a great fear and consternation; but possessed with such a vein, or gift of poetry, that he left the sheep and went about the country, making songs upon all occasions, and came to be the most famous Bard in all the country in his time.

Henry Vaughan

HIMSELF ON HIMSELF
(Fifth Philosopher's Song)

A million million spermatazoa,
    All of them alive:
Out of their cataclysm but one poor Noah
    Dare hope to survive.

And among that billion minus one
    Might have chanced to be
Shakespeare, another Newton, a new Donne –
    But the One was Me.

Shame to have ousted your betters thus,
    Taking ark while the others remained outside!
Better for all of us, froward Homunculus,
    If you'd quietly died!

Aldous Huxley

HOW PLEASANT TO KNOW MR LEAR

How pleasant to know Mr Lear!
  Who has written such volumes of stuff!
Some think him ill-tempered and queer,
  But a few think him pleasant enough.

His mind is concrete and fastidious,
  His nose is remarkably big;
His visage is more or less hideous,
  His beard it resembles a wig.

He has ears, and two eyes, and ten fingers,
  Leastways if you reckon two thumbs;
Long ago he was one of the singers,
  But now he is one of the dumbs.

He sits in a beautiful parlour,
  With hundreds of books on the wall;
He drinks a great deal of Marsala,
  But never gets tipsy at all.

He has many friends, laymen and clerical;
  Old Foss is the name of his cat;
His body is perfectly spherical,
  He weareth a runcible hat.

When he walks in a waterproof white,
  The children run after him so!
Calling out, 'He's come out in his night-
  Gown, that crazy old Englishman, oh!'

He weeps by the side of the ocean,
  He weeps on the top of the hill;
He purchases pancakes and lotion,
  And chocolate shrimps from the mill.

He reads but he cannot speak Spanish,
  He cannot abide ginger-beer;
Ere the days of his pilgrimage vanish,
  How pleasant to know Mr Lear!

Edward Lear

AFTERWARDS

When the Present has latched its postern behind my tremulous stay,
    And the May month flaps its glad green leaves like wings,
Delicate-filmed as new-spun silk, will the neighbours say,
    'He was a man who used to notice such things'?

If it be in the dusk when, like an eyelid's boundless blink,
    The dewfall-hawk comes crossing the shades to alight
Upon the wind-warped upland thorn, a gazer may think,
    'To him this must have been a familiar sight.'

If I pass during some nocturnal blackness, mothy and warm,
    When the hedgehog travels furtively over the lawn,
One may say, 'He strove that such innocent creatures should come to
    no harm,
    But he could do little for them; and now he is gone.'

If, when hearing that I have been stilled at last, they stand at the door,
    Watching the full-starred heavens that winter sees,
Will this thought rise on those who will meet my face no more,
    'He was one who had an eye for such mysteries'?

And will any say when my bell of quittance is heard in the gloom,
    And a crossing breeze cuts a pause in its outrollings,
Till they rise again, as they were a new bell's boom,
    'He hears it not now, but used to notice such things'?

Thomas Hardy

The dew-fall hawk – which begins to churr in the evening, in the
dew-fall when the light is going, is the nightjar. Thomas Hardy knew

it well, a bird of the dark heaths and pines of Dorset. He grew up just under such an extent of heath.

Don't think the next poem out of place. About a glow-worm, yes – like earlier pieces; but more about Wordsworth himself and about his wondering and wonderful sister Dorothy, and her habits of delight.

AMONG ALL LOVELY THINGS

Among all lovely things my love had been;
Had noted well the stars, all flowers that grew
About her home; but she had never seen
A Glow-worm, never one, and this I knew.

While riding near her home one stormy night
A single Glow-worm did I chance to espy;
I gave a fervent welcome to the sight,
And from my horse I leapt; great joy had I.

Upon a leaf the Glow-worm did I lay,
To bear it with me through the stormy night:
And, as before, it shone without dismay;
Albeit putting forth a fainter light.

When to the dwelling of my love I came,
I went into the orchard quietly;
And left the Glow-worm, blessing it by name,
Laid safely by itself, beneath a tree.

The whole next day, I hoped, and hoped with fear;
At night the Glow-worm shone beneath the tree:
I led my Lucy to the spot, 'Look here!'
Oh! joy it was for her, and joy for me!

William Wordsworth

I add – Dorothy Wordsworth again – a portrait of her and the way she smiled, from a poem her brother wrote after they had been on a day's excursion together in the mountains.

Why should I fear to say
That, nymph-like, she is fleet and strong,
And down the rocks can leap along
Like rivulets in May?

And she hath smiles to earth unknown;
Smiles, that with motion of their own
Do spread, and sink, and rise;
That come and go with endless play,
And ever, as they pass away,
Are hidden in her eyes.

She loves her fire, her cottage-home;
Yet o'er the moorland will she roam
In weather rough and bleak;
And, when against the wind she strains,
Oh! might I kiss the mountain rains
That sparkle on her cheek.

Take all that's mine 'beneath the moon',
If I with her but half a noon
May sit beneath the walls
Of some old cave, or mossy nook,
When up she winds along the brook
To hunt the waterfalls.

William Wordsworth

WHEN I AM DRUNK

When I am drunk
I'd like to lie on top of stones
On which pinks bloom.

After the Japanese of Bashō

LEAVES FALLING

A yellow shower of leaves is falling continually from all the trees in the country. . . . The consideration of my short continuance here, which was once grateful to me, now fills me with regret. I would live and live always.

William Cowper

TENNYSON WHEN YOUNG

'Tis the place, and all around it, as of old the curlews call,
Dreary gleams about the moorland flying over Locksley Hall;

Locksley Hall, that in the distance overlooks the sandy tracts,
And the hollow ocean-ridges roaring into cataracts.

Many a night from yonder ivied casement, ere I went to rest,
Did I look on great Orion sloping slowly to the West.

Many a night I saw the Pleiads, rising through the mellow shade,
Glitter like a swarm of fire-flies tangled in a silver braid.

Here about the beach I wandered, nourishing a youth sublime
With the fairy tales of science, and the long result of Time;

When the centuries behind me like a fruitful land reposed;
When I clung to all the present for the promise that it closed;

When I dipt into the future far as human eye could see;
Saw the Vision of the world, and all the wonder that would be.

Alfred Tennyson

Tennyson's Lincolnshire: between the wolds, the sheep hills, on one side, and on the other (pages 196–7, 213) the marshes, the dunes, the beaches and the North Sea – though he lived in a parsonage and not in a hall or manor-house.

OVER THE DARK WORLD FLIES THE WIND

Over the dark world flies the wind
 And clatters in the sapless trees,
From cloud to cloud through darkness blind
 Quick stars scud o'er the sounding seas:
I look: the showery skirts unbind:
 Mars by the lonely Pleiades
Burns overhead: with brows declined
 I muse: I wander from my peace,
And still divide the rapid mind
 This way and that in search of ease.

Alfred Tennyson

A DREAM WITHIN A DREAM

I stand amid the roar
Of a surf-tormented shore,
And I hold within my hand
Grains of the golden sand –
How few! yet how they creep
Through my fingers to the deep,
While I weep – while I weep!
O God! can I not grasp
Them with a tighter clasp?
O God! can I not save
One from the pitiless wave?
Is all that we see or seem
But a dream within a dream?

Edgar Allan Poe

Edgar Allen Poe isn't a poet you would go to for poems about nature, or with nature in them. Poems about human nature, yes; about Edgar Allen Poe's nature. So I have put this, not among the sea poems (though I imagine Edgar Allen Poe standing on one of the long Atlantic beaches of the United States), but among the poems about ourselves, more strictly; the poet, again, on himself.

SONG BY A YOUNG SHEPHERD

When the trees do laugh with our merry wit,
And the green hill laughs with the noise of it,
When the meadows laugh with lively green
And the grasshopper laughs in the merry scene,

When the greenwood laughs with the voice of joy,
And the dimpling stream runs laughing by,
When Edessa, and Lyca, and Emilie,
With their sweet round mouths sing ha, ha, he,

When the painted birds laugh in the shade,
Where our table with cherries and nuts is spread;
Come live and be merry and join with me
To sing the sweet chorus of ha, ha, he.

William Blake

IN KERRY

We heard the thrushes by the shore and sea,
And saw the golden stars' nativity,
Then round we went the lane by Thomas Flynn,
Across the church where bones lie out and in;
And there I asked beneath a lonely cloud
Of strange delight, with one bird singing loud,
What change you'd wrought in graveyard, rock and sea,
This new wild paradise to wake for me –
  Yet knew no more than knew, these merry sins
  Had built this stack of thigh-bones, jaws and shins.

J. M. Synge

HER LEGS

Fain would I kiss my Julia's dainty leg,
Which is as white and hairless as an egg.

Robert Herrick

247

ON HIS MISTRESS, THE QUEEN OF BOHEMIA

You meaner beauties of the night,
That poorly satisfy our eyes
More by your number than your light,
You common people of the skies,
    What are you when the moon shall rise?

You curious chanters of the wood,
That warble forth Dame Nature's lays,
Thinking your voices understood
By your weak accents, what's your praise
    When Philomel her voice shall raise?

You violets, that first appear,
By your pure purple mantles known,
Like the proud virgins of the year,
As if the spring were all your own,
    What are you when the rose is blown?

So, when my mistress shall be seen
In form and beauty of her mind,
By virtue first, then choice a queen,
Tell me, if she were not design'd
    Th' eclipse and glory of her kind?

Sir Henry Wotton

Everyone who remembered her as an English princess wrote out Sir Henry Wotton's poem on the Queen of Bohemia. Not sure whether to think of her as the Queen of the Day or the Queen of the Night, some people wrote 'moon', some people wrote 'sun' in the last line of the first verse. My guess would be that Sir Henry Wotton wrote of her as the full moon rising into the sky and putting out the light of the stars and the planets. She was the daughter of James I of England and VI of Scotland and that Queen Anne from Denmark who listened to the Wiltshire shepherds (page 37) singing on the downs. But it wasn't being royal, it wasn't the pathos of being the Winter Queen, who lost her throne after a single winter in Prague, that made people write her poem out: she had grown up as delightful as her mother had been, charming everyone by her gaiety.

GIPSIES

The gipsies seek wide sheltering woods again,
With droves of horses flock to mark their lane,
And trample on dead leaves, and hear the sound,
And look and see the black clouds gather round,
And set their camps, and free from muck and mire,
And gather stolen sticks to make the fire.
The roasted hedgehog, bitter though as gall,
Is eaten up and relished by them all.
They know the woods and every fox's den
And get their living far away from men;
The shooters ask them where to find the game,
The rabbits know them and are almost tame.
The aged women, tawny with the smoke,
Go with the winds and crack the rotted oak.

John Clare

THE GIPSY CAMP

The snow falls deep; the Forest lies alone:
The boy goes hasty for his load of brakes,
Then thinks upon the fire and hurries back;
The Gipsy knocks his hands and tucks them up,
And seeks his squalid camp, half hid in snow,
Beneath the oak which breaks away the wind,
And bushes close with snow, like hovel warm:
There stinking mutton roasts upon the coals,
And the half-roasted dog squats close and rubs,
Then feels the heat too strong and goes aloof;
He watches well, but none a bit can spare,
And vainly waits the morsel thrown away:
'Tis thus they live – a picture to the place;
A quiet, pilfering, unprotected race.

John Clare

These are gipsies in Epping Forest, near London, where John Clare
lived as a patient in his first asylum. The poem was collected from him
by a visiting journalist, who may not have read Clare's handwriting
properly; or Clare himself may not have worked out all the lines. At

any rate the 7th line does remain a little confused. I like this poem for its naming of the gipsies as 'a quiet, pilfering, unprotected race', gipsies not having changed very much except in their substitution of lorries for carts, and old holiday caravans for painted wooden caravans and crouching tents. Clare, when he was a boy, had learned a number of songs from gipsies; and they had taught him to play the violin. 'Brakes' in the second line would be bundles of dry bracken.

THE GIPSY'S CAMP IN THE BLESSED MORNING

A gipsy's camp was in the copse,
Three felted tents, with beehive tops,
And round black marks where fires had been,
And one old waggon painted green,
And three ribbed horses wrenching grass,
And three wild boys to watch me pass,
And one old woman by the fire
Hulking a rabbit warm from wire.
I loved to see the horses bait.
I felt I walked at Heaven's gate,
That Heaven's gate was opened wide
Yet still the gipsies camped outside.

John Masefield

Hulking a rabbit is paunching or bellying it.

THE TRAMP

He eats (a moment's stoppage to his song)
The stolen turnip as he goes along;
And hops along and heeds with careless eye
The passing crowded stage-coach reeling by.
He talks to none, but wends his silent way,
And finds a hovel at the close of day,
Or under any hedge his house is made
He has no calling and he owns no trade.
An old smoked blanket arches o'er his head.
A wisp of straw or stubble makes his bed.
He knows a lawless law that claims no kin
But meet and plunder on and feel no sin –
No matter where they go or where they dwell,
They dally with the winds and laugh at hell.

John Clare

W. H. Davies (page 239, in particular) was for much of his life a tramp, in America, dossing down at nights and spending the winter in prison, and then in England – a tramp eventually with a wooden leg. Clare's poem he would have approved –

No matter where they go or where they dwell,
They dally with the winds and laugh at hell.

Clare as well might have become a tramp, he felt an outcast and homeless even when he had a home, and before he was taken into an asylum; which doesn't mean he was never happy. In Japan, Issa was another poet poor, deprived, a wanderer, and happy as well as miserable.

We are all in a strange situation; which explains poetry. And peculiar or eccentric many of us are, on top or underneath; whether gipsies, tramps, poets, presidents or prime ministers, – or Edward Lear (another wanderer) or Edward Lear's Uncle Arly.

INCIDENTS IN THE LIFE OF MY UNCLE ARLY

I

O My agèd Uncle Arly!
Sitting on a heap of Barley
   Thro' the silent hours of night, –
Close beside a leafy thicket: –
On his nose there was a Cricket, –
In his hat a Railway-Ticket; –
   (But his shoes were far too tight.)

II

Long ago, in youth, he squander'd
All his goods away, and wander'd
   To the Tiniskoop-hills afar.
There on golden sunsets blazing,
Every evening found him gazing, –
Singing, – 'Orb! you're quite amazing!
   'How I wonder what you are!'

III

Like the ancient Medes and Persians,
Always by his own exertions
   He subsisted on those hills, –
Whiles, – by teaching children spelling, –
Or at times by merely yelling, –
Or at intervals by selling
   Propter's Nicodemus Pills.

IV

Later, in his morning rambles
He perceived the moving brambles –
   Something square and white disclose; –
'Twas a First-class Railway-Ticket;
But, on stooping down to pick it
Off the ground, – a pea-green Cricket
   Settled on my uncle's Nose.

Never – never more, – oh! never,
Did that Cricket leave him ever, –
　　Dawn or evening, day or night; –
Clinging as a constant treasure, –
Chirping with a cheerious measure, –
Wholly to my uncle's pleasure, –
　　(Though his shoes were far too tight.)

So for three-and-forty winters,
Till his shoes were worn to splinters,
　　All those hills he wander'd o'er, –
Sometimes silent; – sometimes yelling; –
Till he came to Borley-Melling,
Near his old ancestral dwelling; –
　　(But his shoes were far too tight.)

On a little heap of Barley
Died my agèd uncle Arly,
　　And they buried him one night; –
Close beside the leafy thicket; –
There, – his hat and Railway-Ticket; –
There, – his ever-faithful Cricket; –
　　(But his shoes were far too tight.)

Edward Lear

SOME STIFF, SOME LOOSE, SOME FIRM

Clay, Sand, and Rock, seem of a diff'rent birth:
So men; some stiff, some loose, some firm: All earth!

Barten Holyday

THAT WEAK PIECE OF ANIMATED DUST

> I truly know
> How men are born, and whither they shall go;
> I know that like to silkworms of one year,
> Or like a kind and wronged lover's tear,
> Or on the pathless waves a rudder's dint,
> Or like the little sparkles of a flint,
> Or like to thin round cakes with cost* perfum'd,
> Or fireworks only made to be consum'd;
> I know that such is man, and all that trust
> In that weak piece of animated dust.
> The silkworm droops, the lover's tears soon shed,
> The ship's way quickly lost, the sparkle dead;
> The cake burns out in haste, the firework's done,
> And man as soon as these is quickly gone.
>   Day hath her night; millions of years shall be
> Bounded at last by long eternity.
> The roses have their spring, they have their fall,
> So have the trees, beasts, fowl, and so have all.

William Browne

THE SKULL OF MAN

Gravedigger   Here's a skull now: this skull, has lain in the earth three and twenty years.

Hamlet   Whose was it?

Gravedigger   A whoreson mad fellow's it was; whose do you think it was?

Hamlet   Nay, I know not.

Gravedigger   A pestilence on him for a mad rogue, a' pour'd a flagon of Rhenish on my head once. This same skull sir, this same skull sir, was Yorick's skull, the King's Jester.

Hamlet   This?

Gravedigger   E'en that.

Hamlet   Let me see. Alas, poor Yorick! – I knew him, Horatio: a fellow of infinite jest, of most excellent fancy: he hath born me on his back a thousand times; and now, how abhorred in my imagination it

---

* cost: costmary grown for flavouring.

is! my gorge rises at it. Here hung those lips that I have kist I know not how oft. Where be your gibes now? your gambols? your songs? your flashes of merriment, that were wont to set the table on a roar? Not one now, to mock your own grinning? quite chop-faln? Now get you to my lady's chamber, and tell her, let her paint an inch thick, to this favour she must come. Prithee, Horatio, tell me one thing.

Horatio What's that, my lord?

Hamlet Dost thou think Alexander look'd o' this fashion i' th' earth?

Horatio E'en so.

Hamlet And smelt so? puh.

Horatio E'en so, my lord.

Hamlet To what base uses we may return, Horatio. Why may not imagination trace the noble dust of Alexander, till he find it stopping a bung-hole?

William Shakespeare

THE SPARROW AND THE LIFE OF MAN

[*Edwin, king of Northumbria, called his friends, princes and noblemen together – it was in the year 627, at York – and asked them severally what they thought of the new god who was urged on them from Kent and from Rome. When Coifi, his High Priest, had spoken up for this new teaching, another councillor added his agreement, and said to the king*]

King, if we consider man's life in our time, in comparison with times past of which we know nothing, it seems to me it resembles the quick lonely flight of a sparrow through the mead hall in which you feast in winter with your noblemen and elders. Inside, the fire gives warmth. Outside, wind drives the rain and the snow. The sparrow flits in through one door, then out through the other, passing from winter to winter. For a little while he enjoys good weather. His comfort soon over, he disappears into the night of winter out of which he came. So it is with ourselves. We come for a short space into this world, but where we come from and where we go to are both unknown to us. If this new teaching instructs us in this more certainly, should we not follow it?

From the Latin of the Venerable Bede

AFTER THE WAR

The helmet now an hive for bees becomes,
And hilts of swords may serve for spiders' looms;
    Sharp pikes may make
    Teeth for a rake;
And the keen blade, th' arch enemy of life,
Shall be degraded to a pruning knife.
    The rustic spade
    Which first was made
For honest agriculture, shall retake
Its primitive employment, and forsake
    The rampires steep
    And trenches deep.
Tame conies in our brazen guns shall breed,
Or gentle doves their young ones there shall feed.
    In musket barrels
    Mice shall raise quarrels
For their quarters. The ventriloquious drum,
Like lawyers in vacations, shall be dumb.
    Now all recruits,
    But those of fruits,
Shall be forgot; and th' unarmed soldier
Shall only boast of what he did whilere,
    In chimney's ends
    Among his friends.

If good effects shall happy signs ensue,
I shall rejoice, and my prediction's true.

Ralph Knevet

Written when peace came after the Civil War, and vindictiveness died
away between Englishmen.

TO THE RIVER DUDDON: AFTER-THOUGHT

I thought of Thee, my partner and my guide,
As being past away. – Vain sympathies!
For, backward, Duddon! as I cast my eyes,
I see what was, and is, and will abide;
Still glides the Stream, and shall for ever glide;
The Form remains, the Function never dies;
While we, the brave, the mighty, and the wise,
We Men, who in our morn of youth defied
The elements, must vanish; – be it so!
Enough, if something from our hands have power
To live, and act, and serve the future hour;
And if, as toward the silent tomb we go,
Through love, through hope, and faith's transcendent dower,
We feel that we are greater than we know.

William Wordsworth

UPON HIS DEPARTURE HENCE

Thus I
Pass by,
And die:
As one,
Unknown,
And gone:
I'm made
A shade,
And laid
I' the grave
There have
My cave.
Where tell
I dwell,
Farewell.

Robert Herrick

Index of authors and poems

Index of titles and first words

Acknowledgements

For allowing the inclusion of copyright material thanks are due to: Longman Group Ltd for 'The Frog Prince', and 'Hymn to the Seal', from *Frog Prince and Other Poems* by Stevie Smith; Macmillan & Co Ltd for 'In the Time of the Breaking of Nations', 'Afterwards', 'Snow in the Suburbs', and 'The Comet at Yell'ham', from *Collected Poems by Thomas Hardy*, also 'The Swan', 'The Peacock', 'The Bluetit', and 'The Porpoise', from *Medieval Welsh Lyrics* by J. P. Clancy, also 'Wild Doves Arriving', and 'The Hunt' (The Unicorn), from *A Skull in Salop* by Geoffrey Grigson; The Society of Authors as the literary representative of the Estate of John Masefield, for 'Madonna Lily', 'The Gipsy's Camp in the Blessèd Morning', and 'The Plough Team', from *The Everlasting Mercy* by John Masefield; Mrs Laura Huxley and Chatto & Windus Ltd for 'Fifth Philosopher's Song', and 'Jonah in the Whale', from *The Collected Poetry of Aldous Huxley*; The Clarendon Press, Oxford for eight lines from 'The snow lies sprinkled on the beach', from *Shorter Poems* by Robert Bridges, 1931; M. B. Yeats and Macmillan & Co. for 'He Reproves the Curlew', 'The Cat and the Moon', and 'The Wild Swans at Coole', from *The Collected Poems of W. B. Yeats*; The Literary Trustees of Walter de la Mare, and the Society of Authors as their representative, for 'A Robin', 'All But Blind', 'Five Eyes', 'Ice', 'The Bindweed', 'The Old Summerhouse', and 'The Spotted Flycatcher', from *The Collected Poems of Walter de la Mare*, 1969; Laurence Pollinger Ltd and the Estate of the late Mrs Frieda Lawrence for 'Bat', and 'Kangaroo', from *The Complete Poems of D. H. Lawrence*, published by William Heinemann Ltd; Alfred A. Knopf Ltd and Random House Inc for 'Philomela', by John Crowe Ransom, from *Selected Poems*, published by Eyre & Spottiswoode Ltd; Oxford University Press by arrangement with the Society of Jesus for 'Nothing is so beautiful as Spring', 'Inversnaid', 'Now I am minded to take pipe in hand', 'When the rainbow arching high' (from *Il Mystico*), 'Like a lark to glide aloof' (from *Il Mystico*), 'All as the moth call'd Underwing alighted', 'When-drops-of-blood-and-foam-dapple' (from *May Magnificat*), and Two Fragments about the Stars, from *Poems of Gerard Manley Hopkins* (4th edition), edited by W. B. Gardner and N. H. Mackenzie; Oxford University Press for 'During the long rains in the fifth month' (no. 113), 'I remember a clear morning' (no. 123), 'When crossing a river' (no. 204), from *The Pillow Book of Sei Shónagon*, translated and edited by Ivan Morris; Edna St Vincent Millay for 'The Buck in the Snow'; Granada Publishing Ltd for 'A Brimstone Butterfly', Autumn Mist', 'Last Snow', 'Mist', 'Snow', 'The Fairy Ring', 'The Mountain', 'The Signpost', from *Collected Poems by Andrew Young*, published by Rupert Hart Davis Ltd; The Hokuseido Press for the following haiku from *A History of Haiku*, by R. H. Blyth, 'The summer moon', by Chiyo-Jo; 'The dawn of day', 'Day darkens', and 'The flowers darken', by Gyódai; 'The does', 'Morning glories', 'My hut', 'Note from a bell', 'Out of the nostril', by Issa; 'Oh for a moon', by Kikaku; 'A cold night', by Kyokusai; 'The autumn of wind', by Kyoroku; 'It is a lonely life', by Onitsura; 'The dragonflies', by Rangai, 'The moon is setting', by Sógi, 'All the various stars', 'A crescent moon', by Taigi; 'Sneezing' by Yayū; also from *Senryu*, by R. H. Blyth, 'The earth is whitish', 'A mushroom',' Resting in the mountain pass', and 'When I am drunk', all by Basho; The Nippon Gakujutsu Shinkōkai for 'A single morning glory', and 'The morning breeze', both by Busōn, and Harvest Moon' by Ranetsu, from *Haikai and Haiku*, 1958; Yale University Press for 'Little City', by Robert Horan, from *A Beginning*; New Directions Publishing Corp., New York for 'The hanging raindrops', by the monk Jakuren, from *One Hundred Poems from the Japanese*, translated by Kennwth Rexroth; Nigel Heseltine for 'I do not sleep at night', from *Dafydd ap Gwilym's Selected Poems*, translated by Nigel Heseltine; Mrs H. M. Davis for 'Days that have been', 'A Great Time', 'I am the Poet Davies, William', 'In the Snow', 'P is for Pool', 'Sheep', and 'Sport', from *The Collected Poems of W. H. Davies*, published by Jonathan Cape Ltd; Estate of Robert Frost for 'A Late Walk', 'A Patch of Old Snow', 'Neither Out Far Nor In Deep', and 'The Quest of the Purple-Fringed', from *The Poetry of Robert Frost*, edited by Edward Connery Lathem, published by Jonathan Cape Ltd; Cambridge University Press for three extracts from *Early Celtic Nature Poetry*, by Kenneth Jackson; Faber & Faber Ltd for 'Sligo and Mayo', and 'Woods', by Louis Macniece, from *Collected Poems*, also 'A Jellyfish', 'Bird-Witted', and 'The Wood-Weasel', by Marianne Moore, from *Complete Poems*, also 'The Cherry Tree', 'The Gallows', 'The Hollow Wood', and 'The Owl', by Edward Thomas, from *Collected Poems*.